LUIS DE GÓNGORA

by David William Foster

and Virginia Ramos Foster

Luis de Góngora is recognized today as Spain's most important poet of the seventeenth century and as a major figure in the emergence of a distinctive Baroque literature in Europe. The significance of Góngora's poetic works is well established among literary historians and critics who have gone beyond his fabled linguistic obscurantism and discovered more profound literary values.

This study is essentially intrinsic in approach, and emphasis is placed on an approximation to the structural characteristics of Góngora's major works. The first two chapters concentrate on a small number of well-known and widely-anthologized texts. The analysis of these texts attempts to go beyond general comments of a vague thematic nature to focus on the structural procedures used by the poet in the realization of acknowledgedly excellent poems. Other chapters treat the *Fable of Polyphemus and Galatea* and *The Solitudes,* works considered the highpoints of Góngora's poetry. A final chapter discusses a few more casual poems and provides the first characterization in English of Góngora's only complete drama, a pseudo-classical work that runs counter to the dominant *comedia* of Lope de Vega and his contemporaries.

Góngora's prominence in Baroque poetics and the complexity of his compositions make a presentation of his works difficult to even the specialist in Spanish literature. The focus of this study on major intrinsic features of the poetry of the "Cordoban Swan" is the attempt to induce in the general reader a satisfactory comprehension of his unusual but often inaccessible brilliance.

ABOUT THE AUTHORS

David William Foster is currently Professor of Spanish at Arizona State University. His research interests include pre-modern Spanish poetry, Spanish bibliography, Spanish linguistics, and the contemporary novel of Spain and Argentina. Support for research has come from the U.S. Office of Education, the Fulbright Program in Argentina, the Research Councils of the University of Missouri and Arizona State University, the National Endowment for the Humanities, the American Philosophical Society, and the Social Science Research Council's Joint Committee on Latin American Studies. Professor Foster writes frequent reviews on River Plate literature for *Books Abroad* and is a member of the Bibliography Committee of Spanish 6 and 7 sections of the Modern Language Association. He is the author of the Twayne World Authors Series volumes on *The Marquis de Santillana* and *The Early Spanish Ballad*.

Virginia Ramos Foster is currently Professor of Spanish at Phoenix College. She has collaborated with David William Foster on bibliographic publications for the University of Washington Press, Scarecrow Press and the Universidad de Puerto Rico. In 1970 she was awarded a grant by the Organización de Estados Americanos for research in Buenos Aires. Professor Foster also serves as a Western regional consultant for the Junior College Board of the National Endowment for the Humanities.

TWAYNE'S WORLD AUTHORS SERIES

A Survey of the World's Literature

Sylvia E. Bowman, Indiana University

GENERAL EDITOR

SPAIN

Gerald Wade, Vanderbilt University

EDITOR

Luis de Góngora

(TWAS 266)

TWAYNE'S WORLD AUTHORS SERIES (TWAS)

The purpose of TWAS is to survey the major writers--novelists, dramatists, historians, poets, philosophers, and critics—of the nations of the world. Among the national literatures covered are those of Australia, Canada, China, Eastern Europe, France, Germany, Greece, India, Italy, Japan, Latin America, the Netherlands, New Zealand, Poland, Russia, Scandinavia, Spain, and the African nations, as well as Hebrew, Yiddish, and Latin Classical literature. This survey is complemented by Twayne's United States Authors Series and English Authors Series.

The intent of each volume in these series is to present a critical-analytical study of the works of the writer; to include biographical and historical material that may be necessary for understanding, appreciation, and critical appraisal of the writer; and to present all material in clear, concise English—but not to vitiate the scholarly content of the work by doing so.

LUIS de GÓNGORA

DAVID WILLIAM FOSTER
Arizona State University

and

VIRGINIA RAMOS FOSTER
Phoenix College

Twayne Publishers, Inc. :: New York

Library of Congress Catalog Card Number 72-13367

MANUFACTURED IN THE UNITED STATES OF AMERICA

Preface

In consonance with the fundamental orientation of the Twayne World Author Series, this examination of the literature of Luis de Góngora, the most important poet of seventeenth-century Spain, is essentially intrinsic. Such a focus is particularly appropriate in the case of Góngora, for since his "rediscovery" in 1927, the third centenary of his death, a quite respectable share of Góngora studies have been intrinsically oriented under the aegis of Dámaso Alonso, currently President of the Royal Spanish Academy, whose dozens of studies have exercised an incalculable influence on several generations of scholars. The desire of the poets involved in the rediscovery of 1927 to understand the relationship between their works and those of the seventeenth century and the desire of scholars to pin down the concrete details of the emerging question of Baroque vs. Renaissance led to the development of close textual analyses of the poetry of Góngora and other major figures of the century in question.

Nevertheless, in retrospect one must, in all candor, recognize a two-pronged weakness of research that has spanned almost half a century. In the first place, by virtue of the overwhelming influence of European schools of language theory of the period, intrinsic studies meant almost exclusively stylistics, and some of Dámaso Alonso's most sophisticated contributions concern the fascinating linguistic components of Góngora's work. However, aside from those instances when stylistic features border on more pervasive issues of poetic organization, such as in the case of some rhetorical formulas, very little work has been done in the area of poetic structure, in the sense of the latter as the organic "mechanism" or unity of a composition. Only recently has European literary criticism seen the emergence of structuralist methods which deal, not just with the unique literary style of literature, but with its organizational "wholeness" as well. In the case of Góngora, this is untilled acreage.

The other serious weakness of seventeenth-century studies, and with particular reference to Góngora, has been, when the balance sheet is cast, the failure to enunciate persuasively a meaningful distinction between the Renaissance (roughly, the late-fifteenth and sixteenth centuries in the Peninsula) and a putative Baroque (the seventeenth century). René Wellek, after a painstaking review of research and opinion in his famous article (see Bibliography), proceeds with the acceptable assumption that the term Baroque is valid because the trained reader does perceive a difference between the seventeenth century and the preceding Renaissance, but finds that he must conclude with a rather cynical assessment of the success of attempts to date at precise characterizations on either stylistic, ideological, or stylistico-ideological grounds. And after one has absorbed with great difficulty Ernst Robert Curtius' detailings of the debts of the Baroque on all three fronts to the literature of late Roman Antiquity and the High Middle Ages (see Bibliography), he cannot help but despair at finding anything tangibly or objectively unique about seventeenth-century literature, although he may nevertheless continue to sense intuitively its uniqueness.

While we cannot pretend to untangle this Gordian knot of European literature history—and indeed there are many who either feel that it has been in fact untangled or that its existence is trivial, although we are unable to take easy comfort in such disconcern—our study of the major works of Luis de Góngora does aspire to providing the critical alternatives of a structuralist interpretation. Perhaps it will be through the suggestion of such alternatives, structuralist and otherwise, that the literary scholar will have at his disposal bases for a more satisfactory resolution of the question of the Baroque. This examination of the poetry of Góngora, aside from the task of providing an accurate and revealing commentary, will find inevitable the issue of what contributions can be made by the intrinsic approach of structuralist criticism to an academic characterization of the nature of Baroque poetry.

A note concerning the texts. The student familiar with Góngora will see mostly familiar titles among the works discussed. Góngora, like many writers of any period, left a good many compositions. But, like any "classic," a handful have come to be accepted as cornerstones of his achievement. It should go without saying that a study such as this must be a showcase of that achievement; the longer poems, a number of sonnets and ballads—these are all

Portrait by Diego Velázquez

LUIS de GÓNGORA

significant works, and we feel compelled to devote to them the space which they deserve. After all, it is only through an in-depth study of a poet's works that his "inner" genius is made clear; this is even truer in the case of the Baroque complexities of Góngora's works.

The texts of Chapters 2, 3, and part of 6 are from the edition of the *Obras completas* edited by J. Millé y Giménez cited in the Bibliography; Millé's numbering and dating of each text is noted. The texts of Chapters 4 and 5 are from the respective editions by Dámaso Alonso cited in the Bibliography.

We regret that, because of space limitations, we have been unable to treat representative *letrillas* and the only completed drama, *Las firmezas de Isabela.*

Contents

Chronology

1561 July 11: Birth of Luis de Góngora y Argote in Córdoba, the fourth son of Francisco de Argote and Leonor Góngora.[1]

1576 Góngora begins to study at the University of Salamanca and takes minor orders.

1580 Góngora leaves the University of Salamanca without a degree. His first poetic work is published in Gómez Tapia's translation of Camões' *Os Lusiadas (The Lusiads).*

1584 A sonnet of Góngora's appears in the preliminaries to the *Austriada (Austriad)* of Juan Rufo.

1585 Takes deacon's orders and becomes prebendary of Córdoba Cathedral, a post vacated by his maternal uncle, Francisco. Cervantes praises the poetic genius of the young Góngora in "El Canto de Caliope" ("Caliope's Song") in *La Galatea (Galatea).* Also, Góngora writes his first masterpiece, the sonnet to Córdoba.

1588 His bishop, Francisco Pacheco, accuses him of poor conduct and negligence in carrying out his clerical duties. Góngora brilliantly defends himself against these charges.

1589 Twelve ballads are published anonymously in the famous anthology, Pedro de Moncayo's *Flor de varios romances nuevos (Flower of Various New Ballads).* Góngora makes several trips to Sevilla.

1590 Goes to Madrid to congratulate the new bishop.

1592 To Madrid again to arrange the royal concession of a prefecture for his nephew.

1593 He experiences an illness of three months in Salamanca. He meets and immediately dislikes Lope de Vega.

1600 Several of his poems are published anonymously in the 1600 *Romancero general (General Songbook of Ballads).*

1603 Goes to the Court at Valladolid and comes into contact with many writers (Cervantes, Espinosa, Vélez de Guevara, Quevedo, etc.). This marks the beginning of the fierce battle over poetics and an enduring enmity towards Quevedo.

1605 Góngora's poems are published in Valladolid in Pedro Espinosa's *Las flores de poetas ilustres (Flowers of Illustrious Poets).*

1604–1608 Góngora continues his life as prebendary in Córdoba.

1609 Visits the Court in Madrid and engages in a strong polemic with

Quevedo; both resort to acerbic invective and personal malignment. Góngora goes to jail, possibly for debts or for his ribald satire.

1610–1615 A period of major poetic activity (rondelets, extended poetic compositions, shorter poems, dramatic works).

1611 Resigns his prebend at Córdoba Cathedral and names his nephew, Don Luis de Saavedra, as his successor. Góngora retires to his country home, the Huerta de Marcos, where he writes *La fábula de Polifemo y Galatea (The Fable of Polyphemus and Galatea)* and also the first part of *Las soledades (The Solitudes)*, his two most important works.

1613 The battle between *conceptismo* (affected poetic language) and *culteranismo* (complex poetic thought) is intensified when Góngora circulates copies of the *Polyphemus* and the *Solitudes.*

1614 Juan de Jáuregui attacks Góngora in his *Antidote Against the Pestilent Poetry of the Solitudes.* In 1614(?) the second part of the *Solitudes* is written.

1615 Don Francisco Fernández de Córdoba, Abad de Rute, defends Góngora's poetry in his *Examination of the Antidote* [by Jáuregui]. Góngora writes a series of carols, "On the Birth of Jesus."

1617 Establishes residence in Madrid and is ordained a priest. He assumes his duties as Chaplain of Honor to Philip III. Also writes "El panegírico al Duque de Lerma" ("Panegyric to the Duke of Lerma") which is never completed.

1618 Writes the "Fábula de Píramo y Tisbe" ("Fable of Pyramus and Thisbe").

1620–1624 Period of intense and mature poetic activity. He produces many ballads, rondelets, and sonnets.

1621 Death of Philip III, who is succeeded by Philip IV. Góngora is plagued by ill health, economic worries, and court intrigues. His dear friend, Rodrigo Calderón, dies on the scaffold.

1622 One of his best friends, the Count of Villamediana, is murdered in August. In October, his good friend, the Count of Lemos, dies. He has lost his best and most influential friends.

1623 In order to pay off some debts, Góngora attempts to arrange the publication of an edition of his poetry, but is unsuccessful.

1625 He is evicted from his home by its new owner, none other than his archenemy, Quevedo. Financial problems overwhelm him and he sells his furniture in order to eat. His nephew ignores his uncle's penury.

1626 Suffers an apoplectic stroke which leaves him paralyzed and amnesic. He returns to Córdoba.

1627 May 23: He dies in Córdoba and is buried in the Chapel of San Bartolomé. All his works are finally published by his devoted friend,

Juan López de Vicuña, as *The Poetic Works of the Spanish Homer.* The Inquisition—with Góngora's disastrous luck in life now afflicting the legacy of his works—prohibits its sale.

1633 First of a series of seventeenth-century reissues of Góngora's complete works.

1921 First modern edition of Góngora's complete works, by the Hispanic Society of America; reprinted in 1970.

1927 "Rehabilitation" of Góngora, on the third centenary of his death, by the young Spanish poets: Salinas, Alonso, García Lorca, Guillén, etc. Composition of Alonso's *La lengua poética . . . (The Poetic Language . . .)*, which is not published until 1935, and the publication of the first edition of Alonso's edition, with prose versions, of the *Solitudes.*

1963 Facsimile edition of the banned 1627 edition of the complete works, two years after the fourth centenary of the poet's birth.

CHAPTER 1

The Life and Times of Luis de Góngora

VIEWING the extensive chronology of Góngora's life, this can be unquestionably described as dramatic, exuberant, and brilliant.[1] He was born of the nobility. He adopted his mother's surname, mostly because he liked its lyrical quality as well as its antepenultimate accent. He was able until near his life's end to pursue an active mental and social life. His student days were a blend of amorous and picaresque adventures, serious scholarship (he became well versed in classical mythology, Latin, Italian, and Portuguese languages and literatures), and artistic accomplishments such as painting, writing, the theater, and music. Indeed, it is said that he was a gifted musical composer and that he was also one of the first to recognize the great talents of the painter El Greco. This multifaceted life-style in his youth was to become for Góngora a permanent mode of activity. Fortunately, he was able to combine his religious obligations and secular interests when he was commissioned to travel throughout Spain on official assignments for the church. He clearly preferred the worldly excitement to be found among the literary and intellectual circles of Madrid and Córdoba over the rather routine, provincial duties of his post at Córdoba's Cathedral. For the most part, his existence was a series of financial as well as political ups and downs, as he lived beyond his means, possessed of a consuming passion for cards and women, socializing with low-class theater people, and pursuing other activities conducive neither to economic stability nor social conformity. However, in 1617 Góngora thought that his luck was to change when he was finally ordained a priest and became the Chaplain of Honor to Philip III. But this experience ultimately resulted in bitter disappointment and failure, mainly due to economic distress, multifarious court intrigues, and Góngora's apparently congenital inability to ally himself with people who could be helpful to him. Despite his disenchantment and the rampant antagonism toward his poetic creativity and innovations, as well as his personal failure to come to any viable terms with his own life, Góngora continued to find an outlet in brilliant poetic expression. His linguistic versatility is patent in the many kinds of poetic forms he practiced: amorous, scurrilous and satirical, pastoral, heroic and religious. Indeed, he has frequently been considered the greatest of Spanish sonneteers. His highly original works began with the more typically Renaissance modes, but as time went on his poetry became progressively more complex, difficult and innovative, reaching a climax in 1613 with the *Polifemo (Polyphemus)* and the *Soledades (Solitudes)*. It is through these great poetic contributions to Spanish literature of the seventeenth century—the cornerstones of his current reputation—that Góngora has secured a foremost place in world literature.

But if Góngora's life was not easy, neither were the times in which he lived. Góngora was part of the fabled Golden Age of Spain—golden that is, for its outstanding letters, not for its political and economic conditions. Spain was at the height of her power under Charles V (1516–1556), a forceful leader who became tired of the vast problems of governing the huge empire and who abdicated in favor of his son, Philip II. This event started the movement towards the well-chronicled decline and decay of the Spanish Empire. Philip entered a long series of wars with everyone, including the Pope, the French, English, Flemish, and others. He suffered a crushing defeat when the Invincible Armada was destroyed in 1588. Philip III (1598–1621), his successor, was also involved in many wars with Ireland, the Low Countries, the Turks, and the Thirty Years War on the Catholic side. Philip was a weak ruler, incapable of coping with the complexities which understandably beset a great world power. He played an unfortunate political game of favorites, thus assigning authority to his chosen ones like the Duke of Lerma. Part of Góngora's trouble stemmed unquestionably from his own clumsy attempts to play this game—and he was to outlive many men on whose fortunes he had unwisely staked his own, among them the Duke of Lerma. Philip III's policies were continued under Philip IV (1621–1665). Wars, government by favorites, and an inept management of finances all contributed to the decline of the turbulent milieu in which Góngora lived out his hapless life and yet produced the most important poetic works of the century.

I Conceptismo *vs.* Culteranismo

The seventeenth century, the period of the Baroque in Europe, is often considered—somewhat negatively—as the Age of Affectation. It is a time when literature undergoes two distinct developments in the theory of what constitutes elegant writing: *conceptismo* or the cultivation of subtlety of concepts (ideas), and *culteranismo* (also called *gongorismo*), the cultivation of linguistic difficulty and obscurity.[2] (It would, in passing, be naive to view these two aspects as so distinct as to be unrelated and mutually independent, for frequently writers of the Baroque manifest both tendencies.) The stormy battle over these two tendencies reached a high point in 1613 when Góngora—usually aligned with *culteranismo*—circulated copies of his linguistically complex *Fábula de Polifemo y Galatea (Fable of Polyphemus and Galatea)* and the first part of the *Solitudes.* The literati quickly split into two groups: Quevedo was the major spokesman for *conceptismo* while Góngora headed the *culteranistas.* Thus, it would be profitable to survey the basic meanings of these two aspects or "movements" which produced the most famous polemic in the history of Spanish literature.

Conceptismo, as one permanent legacy of the Middle Ages, is the product of the dialectics of scholastic reasoning whereby intellectuals schooled in theological debate would apply their system to the discussion of other themes like love and honor.[3] Reasoning became a major characteristic of the Provençal writers whose ideas influenced both Italian and Spanish poets, but *conceptismo* also had later peninsular roots in the Salamancan School headed by the poet Fray Luis de León (1528–1591). This group, noted for the dialectic of its Neoplatonic ideas, was preoccupied with the idea and the conceit usually considered inherent in the goals and attitudes of *conceptismo.* Those Baroque writers who adhered to traditional, idiomatic Spanish abhorred linguistic and stylistic obscurity; rather, they sought out brilliant, ingenious thoughts, relying heavily on conceits, antithesis, parallelism, paradox, metaphors, and various types of puns and wordplay.

On the other hand, *culteranismo* or *gongorismo* (Marinism in Italy; euphuism in England; *préciosité* in France; *Schwulst* in Germany) is a movement which appealed rather to a limited audience of cultured intellectuals, steeped in the conventions of classical Antiquity. *Culteranismo* also goes back in history to medieval rhetoric and to the sixteenth-century Sevillan School, which stressed poetic rhetoric, the common denominator of *culteranismo.* The stress on syntactical and lexical innovations sought to make Spanish conform more to Latin. It must be remembered in this regard that during the Renaissance scholars emphasized the superiority of Latin over the vernacular languages—classical Latin was richer in vocabulary and more complex in syntax, while the Romance languages were considered corruptions of Latin, outgrowths of the spoken Vulgar Latin. Like Juan de Mena in the fifteenth century and Herrera in the sixteenth, Góngora and his followers strove to enrich Spanish as a literary medium. They borrowed and invented new words from Latin and Greek (neologisms), distorted syntax (hyperbaton, Greek accusative, ablative absolute, etc.), suppressed the definite article (an invention of Vulgar Latin). They used striking and ingenious metaphors and epithets and resorted to extensive references to classical mythology as well as to exotic non-Hispanic geographical locations. Although they cultivated an ornate and pompous style, these writers did demand high artistic standards and did enrich Spanish vocabulary to such an extent that many of their innovations are in prevalent use today: *ostentar* (to make a show), *canoro* (melodious), *celestial* (celestial), *aplauso* (applause), *fulgor* (splendor) are but a few of the now common words which were originally introduced by the *culteranistas.*[4]

Perhaps a way of marking the different goals and yet potential interrelationships between these two late-Renaissance tendencies is to see *conceptismo* in simplistic terms as content and *culteranismo* as form. Together they emphasize the degree to which poetry in both of its essential and inseparable aspects was unyieldingly committed to the unique, the brilliant, the lyrical, and to the ineffable—to the *no sé qué,* to use one of the most common stylistic commonplaces of the period.

II *Poetic Allegiances and Controversies*

As Góngora continued to engage in experimentation with varying poetic forms and linguistic innovations, many poets allied themselves with his aesthetics and revitalized the tradition of learned poetry, a poetry basically oriented towards an intellectual elite. (And many members of that elite dared not confess that they did not comprehend the poetic experience offered by these poets.) Among the best-known disciples of *gongorismo* were the Conde de Villamediana, Pedro Soto de Rojas, and Hortensio Félix Paravicino y Arteaga.[5]

The Conde de Villamediana was not only Góngora's patron, but also a close friend; both men shared the same literary interests as well as a passion for adventure, women, and gambling. Villamediana closely imitated Góngora to the extent that he included entire verses of the master in his compositions—this was not considered plagiarism but rather a public tribute of deep appreciation for his friend. Villamediana was especially inspired by Góngora's sonnets, which he tried to imitate stylistically, attempting also to capture their mood and tone.

If the best of Villamediana was due to the inspiration of Góngora's sonnets, the best of Soto de Rojas were the results of the influence of the *Solitudes*. Renowned for his *Paraíso cerrado para muchos, jardines abiertos para pocos (A Paradise Closed to Many; Gardens Open to a Few)* 1652, Pedro Soto de Rojas indulged in a difficult, cerebral type of poetry which reflected Góngora's own richness of language and love of conceit, image, rhythm, and sound. Like Góngora, Soto de Rojas has undergone a significant reevaluation in the twentieth century. The late Federico García Lorca thought him to be a poet of major stature, superior to Góngora in technique and subject matter, while Gerardo Diego, also a poet of our own time, finds him to be a more human and sensitive artist.[6]

A difficult dimension of *gongorismo* is to be seen in another facet of Spanish rhetoric: sacred oratory. Hortensio Paravicino, court preacher during the reigns of Philip III and Philip IV, was a devotee of a difficult, affected style, and he applied complicated literary techniques to the sermon, which was not primarily a literary form. Imbued with so-called "Baroque energy," Paravicino found success in the pulpit, where he earned his reputation as a gifted preacher whose sermons reflected an erudite concern with images, similes, metaphors, and allegories. As an ardent admirer of Góngora, he eulogized him frequently in his poetic compositions.

III *Personal Attacks on Góngora: Quevedo's Enmity*

Góngora's enemies were many during this literary "civil war" of some fifty years duration (1613–1662), when the heated polemics reached comic as well as serious proportions between the "Swans" (the *culteranistas*—Góngora was known as the "Cordoban Swan") and the "Geese" (the *conceptistas*). The worst attacks of the "Geese" (at least vis-à-vis the "Cordoban Swan") came from Quevedo and Lope de Vega, two of the most brilliant writers of the period.

Quevedo, twenty years younger than Góngora, was the major spokesman against Góngora and his followers in this momentous battle. Although Quevedo wrote in an ingenious and complicated fashion, he fought *gongorismo* on behalf of a simple, direct style, which he himself never mastered. Nevertheless, Quevedo objected to Góngora's pedantry, to his obscurity of language and allusion, and to his unorthodox usage of the Spanish language. The two artists snapped and snarled and taunted each other mercilessly, but it was Quevedo who was especially vitriolic and sarcastic in his *ad hominem* insults. Thus, Góngora was ridiculed for his long nose and was accused of having a Jewish background and of being a ghetto rabbi. Quevedo even advised him to give up writing:

Yo te untaré mis versos con tocino,
porque no me los muerdas, Gongorilla,
perro de los ingenios de Castilla,
docto en pullas, cual mozo de camino.
¿Apenas hombre, sacerdote indino,
que aprendiste sin christus la cartilla,
hecho carnero en Córdoba y Sevilla
y bufón en la corte, a lo divino.
¿Por qué censuras tú la lengua griega,
siendo sólo rabí de la judía
cosa que tu nariz no lo niega?
No escribas versos más, por vida mía;
que aun aquesto de escribas se te pega
pues tienes de sayón la rebeldía.[7]

(I will smear my verses with bacon for you, so that you'll not bite into them, dear Góngora, dog of the geniuses of Castile, gifted in obscenities like any wandering kid. Barely a man, unworthy as a clergyman, you earned your certificate of orders [or, you learned your primer] without *christus* [Christ?, that which is annointed?]; you became mutton (i.e., a simpleton) in Córdoba and Sevilla and a fool at Court, in a divine way. Why do you criticize the Greek language, being only a Jewish rabbi, a fact which your nose cannot deny? Don't write any more verses, upon my soul! Even this business about scribes [pun on "don't write" and the word for "Jewish scribes"] sticks to you, for you have rebelliousness as your ugly face.)[8]

Upon publication of the *Solitudes* and the *Polyphemus*, Quevedo seized the opportunity to lash out again against Góngora's bombastic style and obscurity:

¿Qué captas, nocturnal, en tus canciones,
Góngora bobo, con crepusculallas,
si cuando anhelas más garcivolles,
las reptilezas más y subterpones?
Microcósmote Dios de inquiridiones,
y quieres te investiguen por medallas
como priscos estigmas o antiguallas,
por desitinerar vates tirones.
Tu forasteridad es tan eximia
que te ha de detractar el que te rumia,
pues ructas viscerable cacoquimia,
farmacofolorando como numia
si estomacabundancia das tan nimia,
metamorfoseando el arcadumia.[9]

(What do you captivate, nocturnally, in your songs, stupid Góngora, by crepusculating them, if the more you yearn to heron-fly them the more you reptilize and subterpose them? I microcosmate you God of classical manuals, and you want to be searched for medals like ancient stigmata or relics, in order to confuse the novice poets. Your foreignity is so noteworthy that he who ruminates you must denigrate you, for you eructate intestinable dungistry, pharmacologizing like a Numian (?), if you yield so little stomach-abundance, metamorphosizing the aqueductry.)[10]

Quevedo's final triumph came when he was able to evict Góngora (then sixty-four years old and suffering ill health and penury) after he bought the house in which Góngora was living. And to add insult to injury, Quevedo publicized the necessity of having to purify and perfume the place from the "pestilence of the *Polyphemus* and the *Solitudes*." Quevedo said that he had to burn like purifying incense the works of Garcilaso (a sixteenth-century poet who wrote with a very clear Renaissance style). This hatred of Quevedo for Góngora continued well beyond the latter's death in 1627.

IV . *Góngora and Lope de Vega*

Góngora's altercations with Lope de Vega, who lived near him in Madrid, were somewhat milder. Lope, sensitive to Góngora's imagination and creativity, often praised him in his works. But the "Cordoban Swan" despised Lope and aggressively criticized his art as well as his stormy love life. When Lope published his epic poem *Jerusalem Conquered,* Góngora insulted him by writing his attack on the poem in a Negro dialect. But still, despite these exchanges, Lope deeply respected Góngora's talent and confessed that he was not always attacking Góngora directly, but rather those who poorly imitated him. In fact, Lope viewed Góngora as an innovator in Spanish letters by calling his poetry "new poetry" and his style, a "new style." Indeed, Góngora spoke a new language for Lope. When the controversial and famous master died, Lope wrote an eulogistic sonnet in the former's learned style:

A LA MUERTE DE DON LUIS DE GÓNGORA

Despierta, ¡oh Betis!, la dormida plata
y, coronado de ciprés, inunda
la docta patria, en Sénecas fecunda,
todo el cristal en lágrimas desata;
repite soledades, y dilata
por campos de dolor vena profunda,
única luz, que no dejó segunda;
al polifemo ingenio Atropos mata.
Góngora ya la parte restituye
mortal al tiempo, ya la culta lira
en cláusula final a voz incluye.
Ya muere y vive: que esta sacra pira
tan inmortal honor le constituye
que nace fénix donde cisne expira.[11]

(ON THE DEATH OF DON LUIS DE GÓNGORA. Oh, Betis, your sleeping silver awakens and, crowned with cypress, inundates the learned fatherland, fecund in Senecas, freeing all its crystal in tears. It repeats solitudes, and spreads out over fields of grief a deep streak, an only light which allowed no seconds, and Atropos kills the ingenious Polyphemus [i.e., Góngora]. Góngora is already restoring to time its immortal part; he is already including vocally in a final clause the cultured lyre. He is now both dead and alive, for this sacred pyre represents for him so immortal an honor that a Phoenix is born from where a Swan [i.e., Góngora] expires.[12]

V *The Attitude of the Literary Theorists*

The heated controversy between the poets also pervaded the literary criticism of the times. Spanish theorists concerned themselves with serious discussions of the fundamentals of art as well as personal commentary on the artists. Important issues centered on the question of imitation, whether it was to be classical or Italian in focus, on the matter of rhetoric and poetic language and erudition and the value of intellectual, esoteric art.[13] Even Góngora was conscious of poetic theory and adhered to his own principles, stating that his stylistic obscurity was an intentional goal which served an aesthetic purpose.[14] Aware of his poetic talents, Góngora recognized the fact that he had brought Spanish to the same heights of perfection attained by the Latin language. In 1624 one pro-Góngora commentator, Díaz de Rivas, synthesized in detail the eleven principal objections that critics had found with Góngora's style:[15] (1) too many unusual words; (2) the frequent use of tropes; (3) too many inversions of words and ideas; (4) an obscure, complex style; (5) the harshness of metaphors (in the sense of depersonalization?); (6) an uneven style; (7) the mixture of humble words with sublime ones; (8) the frequent repetition of the same words and phrases (Góngora had his favorite words and stylistic constructions (i.e., "not A, but B"; "A when not B"; *purpúreo* [purple], *joven* [young], *crepúsculos* [twilights], etc.); (9) hyperbole and great exaggeration; (10) the length of some periods; (11) redundancy and repetition of expression. Pedro Díaz de Rivas, however, went on to defend Góngora against the critics and proclaimed him to be the most outstanding artist in the realm of poetry; in particular, Díaz de Rivas adhered to and respected the principle of poetic license.

The distinguished Humanist, Pedro de Valencia, in his famous "Letter of Censure," appreciated Góngora's literary skill but nevertheless opposed his extravagant style, licentious metaphors, and some of the wordplay in the *Polyphemus* and the *Solitudes*.

Góngora in this case tried to please his friend and critic, and he did revise a few passages that were particularly displeasing to Valencia.

One of the commentators who were more hostile to Góngora's work was Juan de Jáuregui. His *Antidote Against the Solitudes* (1613–1614) is a long, critical document that subscribes to no particular aesthetic orientation; at best, the work can be described as a vitriolic diatribe against Góngora personally and professionally. If one reads Jáuregui, the extent to which he misunderstood Góngora becomes apparent. But ten years later, in 1624, he did come to contribute an important work, his *Poetic Discourse*, which is considered a hallmark of literary criticism for its more coherent and sophisticated evaluation of *culteranismo* than was the *Antidote*.

Francisco Fernández de Córdoba, Abad de Rute, joined the fight and defended Góngora in his *Examination of the Antidote* (1615?), where he takes issue with the various critics and upholds the new poetic sensibility with which Góngora was infusing Spanish letters. He maintains the belief that Góngora is worthy of being compared to the best of the classic poets and finds the Spaniard to be particularly brilliant in the *Solitudes*, above all in five extraordinary passages: his description of rustic life beginning with "Oh fortunate retreat . . ." (see below, pp. 148ff.), the ocean voyage, the games, the wedding song, and the words of the wanderer in the second *Solitude*.

VI *Góngora and the Baroque*

As a Baroque poet, Góngora labored under what can only be called a doctrine of pedantry, and unlike Shakespeare and Milton, he held little interest in a common idiom or in the masses. But Góngora is a modern poetic rebel in that he fought to enrich and to give new poetic awareness to the poetic experience, and the Spanish theorists who were his defenders called him the "Spanish Homer," precisely because he was the one poet whose work could equal the literature produced in Greece, Rome, or Italy. Indeed, Góngora brought to a culmination the "new Renaissance poetry" in the Peninsula.[16]

Beyond this, one must acknowledge the degree to which Góngora turned away from the standard concept of imitation to develop a whole new style of poetic reality rooted in the concept of the poem as object, as the genesis of substantive art. Borrowing heavily from the classical ideas of mimesis, late fifteenth- and sixteenth-century poets strove to create a naturalistic world in their compositions. Although it was principally an idealized naturalism, its emphasis was on the image and the degree to which the poet was able to capture in his lines a reflection of the balance of the harmony of Nature. The poem opened up a world which was only somewhat emphasized or exaggerated, and attention was directed to the poet's skill in making us see and feel people, places, and things in his poems. Verisimilitude and acceptability were stressed: the poem was a mirror held up to Nature and the human soul. Baroque poetry—Góngora's works—however, breaks that mirror and attempts to create a whole new world of sensation and experience in the poem. *Agudeza* (intellectual sharpness), *ingenio* (wit), *concepto* (conceit), as immortalized in Baltasar Gracián's 1642 treatise on poetic theory, define the limits of this art of creation.[17] No more is the poet compelled to impress his audience with imitation and recreation, but rather the new aesthetic was to startle with extravagance, to bring a new horizon of poetic reality. It is Góngora's art and that of the bulk of the poets of the Baroque that broke the bonds of harmony, verisimilitude, credibility and natural reality, bringing forth out of chaos a new totally creative patterning of relationships, a new Nature individually interpreted, and supposedly far superior in its complexity to the trite, mimetic *loci amoeni* of the previous age.

This effort to construct a poem which is an objective monument to its own reality characterizes the tremendous tension of Baroque artistry, especially as we find it in Góngora's poetry, and explains the desire to overcome the now-platitudinous Renaissance balance and harmony and to experiment with the results which the extravagant, the unusual, and the unknown bring. Baroque art is no less ordered than Renaissance art; it is simply a matter of different rules of ordering, different concepts of balance, integration, development, etc. Thus, this chaotic tension in a Baroque work in the final analysis yields no less an explicable style and structure than does, say, Garcilaso's "First Eclogue."

Although Baroque poetry offers, to a certain extent, a new range of themes, mostly based on religious issues, including disillusionment and the relativity of reality and the flux of time, Góngora's poetry treats many basic topics that are found in the Renaissance. To a certain degree, love is a common theme, but Nature is really the dominant protagonist of the poet's major works. Recent opinion has centered on the Neoplatonism of the *Polyphemus* and the *Solitudes* and argues for seeing these works as elaborations of the theme of the harmony of Nature upset and destroyed by disruptive elements, particularly by the grotesque in Nature itself *(Polyphemus)* or by the action of men insensitive to her blessings (the *Solitudes*). To this extent, Góngora would be pursuing a typical Baroque concern over the harmony and the permanence of a Nature which in his disillusionment he sees threatened by her own destructive forces. Gone is the calm assurance and tranquility of the *beatus ille.* Nature is no longer stable, but has become frighteningly turbulent and mutable. Through the intense language of Baroque poetry, the complex system of allusions, conceitful analogies and "painterly" development,[18] Góngora's mature poetry in its creative relative unity of the whole strives for an expressive correlation with the theme, a correlation absent in Renaissance poetry, where even tragedy and misfortune are rendered in the same tranquil, ordered manner of an ultimate harmony.

This expressive correlation of language in its attempt to render in the objectified poem the tension of the subject matter is one of the fundamental characteristics of Góngora's Baroque poetic rhetoric. "Hermetic" is a term frequently applied to this rhetoric, and it is an apt one to the extent that it underlines the way in which language becomes the complex and the immutable fabric of the poem as artistic creation. The difficult interrelation, the neologisms, hyperbaton, allusions and analogies, the recurring hypotactic and paratactic structures, all constitute a necessary and integral part of a poetic theory that sees the composition as more than the mere harmonious balancing of words and stanzas; it is a unique expressive object in and of itself, a new reality with its own solid and inextricable architecture. It is on this basis that we can and must understand the Baroque poet's extreme concern with density and complexity of expression, for thereby does he bequeath to his poem a never-ending pattern of meaning and its own unmistakable brilliant uniqueness.

This never-ending, ever-changing pattern of meaning derives largely from the increased connotation brought to the poem by the poet's use of a wide variety of rhetorical resources and devices, largely the classically based neologism and the extravagant syntax establishing new and audacious semantic and grammatical relationships for Spanish. The use of expressive formulas such as *no A, sino B* (not A, but B), *si A, no B* (if A, not B), *ya A, ya B* (now A, now B), and so on, not only reinforces the essential thematic and stylistic tension, but also serves to broaden our understanding of the range of possibilities, meanings, combinations, and antitheses of what is being presented. The extensive use of parallelistic structures also contributes to the poet's goal of interrelating as much as possible and proving vividly to his reader that reality is neither static nor linear, but rather shifting, recursive, plurivalent in significance, and, above all, dramatic.

Góngora's poetry is dedicated to revealing to us, in theme and in structure and style, the tremendous complexity of reality as the mind is capable of seeing it, analyzing it, and portraying it for another mind. The concept of the conceit underlines this theory of a reality which is multifaceted and intensely difficult to interpret in its refusal to yield a unilateral meaning. The Baroque aesthetic as we see it in the poetry of Góngora, although we may feel at times that his production is unusually and unnecessarily mannerist in its attempt to explore a radically new concept of literary experience, is nevertheless unquestionably committed to the exploration of art as man's highest form for realizing and giving shape to his experience of life as a human soul and as a human intellect.

CHAPTER 2

The Ballads

GÓNGORA left ninety-four *romances* (ballads in octosyllabic verse) and *romancillos* (ballads in shorter verse, usually hexasyllabic); in addition, another eighteen are attributed to him. Together they constitute between one-fifth and one-fourth of his entire poetic production and are usually agreed to have been composed throughout his life. The earliest date from 1580, the beginning of his career at nineteen, and the latest from 1626, the year of his apoplectic disablement and one year before his death. Thus, as in the case of the sonnets (see our next chapter), Góngora devoted full creative attention to the ballads, and, as is also the case with many other poems, one can perceive neither a direct line of development from facile "pseudopopular" compositions to complex *culteranista* tours de force, nor any general grouping of types and themes. Indeed, some of the earliest, such as the first text examined below, reveal on the one hand the distinct absorption of popular-traditional motifs, and on the other a superficial expressive lucidity which masks Baroque stylistic traits associated with the poet's most difficult poems.[1]

Thus, a chronological reading of the ballads presents a miscellany of texts which, however, can be said to divide themselves into two not-so-distinct groups. On one side we can place the satirico-jocular poems, rude and often scatological in language, burlesque and abusive in content. With notably few exceptions, a study of Góngora's poetry interested basically in significant poetic attainments rather than in the relative typological categories of a "works-and-man" study will dismiss most of these compositions as thin and irrelevant to literature as significant art. True, as a whole these pieces demonstrate a certain streak of black humor *avant la lettre* in the seventeenth century, and Francisco de Quevedo was able to achieve a high literary level out of what, one must assert frankly, rarely rises above bathroom humor in the case of Góngora. The direct point of coincidence with the Baroque *Weltanschauung* is, of course, a certain crumbling of the cosmic vision that C. S. Lewis is to call the "discarded image"[2] and a most pronounced tendency to invert former values that were coming to be seen as obnoxious clichés. Thus, Otis Green may see the continuity of the medieval courtly love tradition through the amorous poetry of Quevedo,[3] but when the latter is also able to pen an encomium of a woman's *ojo de culo [oculum culi]*, is this not but the outrageous extension of the *topoi* (commonplaces) concerning the beloved's ideal physical attributes? Góngora, in any case, does not go far poetically in this respect, and the only humorous ballads that deserve close examination are those that mock the received mythological tradition, as the ballad on Pyramus and Thisbe[4] (a little more than five hundred lines long) or one on Hero and Leander.

The second set of ballads includes some of Góngora's most famous—and most spectacularly successful—poetic compositions. While it is not easy to winnow nonserious from serious works, there is a majority of ballads that evince a more recognizable aspiration to significant literature. Although we don't want to enter here into the thicket of problems associated with typological classification, it is only fair to the general reader to make some comment on the nature of the ballad in Spain and the relationship of Góngora's individual compositions to a vigorous and widespread tradition of popular-traditional, semipopular and learned-professional poetry.

I *The Evolution of the Ballad*

The anonymous ballad tradition develops in Spain during the fourteenth and fifteenth centuries, producing an enormous quantity of oral compositions, many of outstanding literary merit. These began to be put down in writing and circulated among the court poets in the late fifteenth and early sixteenth centuries.[5] For a number of reasons, but basically through a humanistic interest in traditional and popular literature as well as in the Italian and classical influences, and the very intrinsic merit of the early unsigned ballads, many poets of the Spanish Renaissance manifest a strong interest in the ballad, both as a verse form and as a type of narrative format characterized by abrupt beginnings and endings and portrayals of intense dramatic concentration in as few lines as possible. Indeed, a "constant" of Spanish literature, much like the

Alexandrine of French literature, has been the persistence of the ballad form throughout the centuries among professional poets (the original oral tradition has also survived independently, of course) ever since the publication in 1600 of the *Romancero nuevo (Songbook of New Ballads)*. This anthology, which contained a number of Góngora's works, gathered together the production of ballads by the professional, learned court poets stimulated by the late medieval oral tradition; it also constituted a support in the further development of the genre throughout the new century.

Góngora's ballads represent a miscellany of themes and styles, not to mention examples of relative approximation to or distancing from the vague norm that Spanish literary historians sense as a constant of balladry, whether oral and anonymous, or printed and signed. (For example, Federico García Lorca's 1927 *Romancero gitano [Gypsy Ballads]* adheres strikingly to this centuries-old norm and contains, perhaps as a direct result, some of the most important poems written in Spanish in this century.) Going beyond our rather simplistic distinction—based more on questions of taste than on literary typology—Oreste Frattoni recognizes for Góngora ten types of ballads: those to be sung, compositions on Moorish themes, poems concerning captives (usually Christians by Moors), ballads on chivalrous themes, descriptive-allegorical ballads, eulogies of cities, occasional compositions, amorous poems, sacred poems, and satiric-burlesque ballads.[6]

The discussion which follows is not concerned with illustrating each of Frattoni's categories. The critic must be honest both toward the poet and toward the reader: the bulk of Góngora's ballads make up the weakest segment of his total work. Indeed, one recent critic would have us gloss over quite a large portion of the amorous poems written along the lines of the courtly love tradition.[7] Nevertheless, there is a radical distinction to be made between "averaging out" Góngora's total production of ballads and singling out specific works as representing literary art of the highest sort, no matter what genre they may belong to. For this reason, the choice of texts to be studied in this chapter can come as no surprise to the reader familiar with Spanish anthologies.

II A Popular Romancillo

It is fitting that we begin with a poem that is undoubtedly one of Góngora's most popular, one of his earliest (1580), and one which reveals the best of the Renaissance-Baroque harmonistics between the traditional and the learned. The ballad "La más bella niña" ("The Prettiest Girl") is known in at least three quite distinct versions.[8] The text we give is generally assumed to be both the latest and the most successful of the three:[9]

	La más bella niña	(The prettiest girl
	de nuestro lugar,	in our village,
	hoy viuda y sola	today a widow and alone,
	y ayer por casar,	and yesterday about to marry,
5	*viendo que sus ojos*	seeing that her eyes [i.e., lover]
	a la guerra van,	are off to the war,
	a su madre dice,	says to her mother,
	que escucha su mal:	who listens to her lament:
10	*Dejadme llorar*	Let me weep
	orillas del mar.	at the shores of the sea.
	Pues me distes, madre,	Since you gave me, mother,
	en tan tierna edad	at so tender an age
	tan corto el placer,	so brief a pleasure,
15	*tan largo el pesar,*	so long a suffering,
	y me cautivastes	and you made me captive
	de quien hoy se va	of him who today is going away
	y lleva las llaves	and taking with him the keys
	de mi libertad.	of my liberty:
20	*Dejadme llorar*	Let me weep
	orillas del mar.	at the shores of the sea.
	En llorar conviertan	Let my eyes change to crying,
	mis ojos, de hoy más,	from today on,
	el sabroso oficio	their delightful occupation
	del dulce mirar	of sweetly looking,
25	*pues que no se pueden*	since they can't
	mejor ocupar,	better occupy themselves,
	yéndose a la guerra	since he is going off to the war
	quien era mi paz.	who was my peace.
	Dejadme llorar	Let me weep
30	*orillas del mar.*	at the shores of the sea.
	No me pongáis freno	Don't hold me back
	ni queráis culpar;	or want to blame me;

	que lo uno es justo	for the one would be proper,
	lo otro por demás.	the other too much.
35	*Si me queréis bien*	If you really love me
	no me hagáis mal;	don't do me ill;
	harto peor fuera	it would be much worse
	morir y callar.	to die and be silent.
	Dejadme llorar	Let me weep
40	*orillas del mar.*	at the shores of the sea.
	Dulce madre mía	Sweet mother mine,
	¿quién no llorará,	who would not weep
	aunque tenga el pecho	even if his heart
	como un pedernal,	were hard as flint,
45	*y no dará voces,*	and who would not cry out,
	viendo marchitar	seeing wither away
	los más verdes años	the greenest years
	de mi mocedad?	of my youth?
	Dejadme llorar	Let me weep
50	*orillas del mar.*	at the shores of the sea.
	Váyanse las noches,	Let the nights be gone,
	pues ido se han	for the eyes are gone
	los ojos que hacían	which used to make
	los míos velar;	mine stay awake;
55	*váyanse, y no vean*	let them be gone and not see
	tanta soledad,	so much loneliness,
	después que en mi lecho	now that my bed
	sobra la mitad.	is half as much too big.
	Dejadme llorar	Let me weep
60	*orillas del mar.*	at the shores of the sea.)[10]

One's first impression from reading the ballad is that of utter artlessness, of a complete and successful imitation of the traditional, anonymous folk poetry. Unlike the ballad of Angélica and Medoro (see below), the ballad of the young girl whose lover has gone to war presents neither linguistic nor conceptual problems. Indeed, even if it weren't good poetry, the text would command some attention for being quite a striking re-creation of the spirit and tone of the medieval Gallaico-Portuguese *cantigas de amigo* (canticles of friends—i.e., lovers), in which the woman laments the solitude caused by her lover's absence. As Bruce Wardropper has shown in his article mentioned above, one can discern, upon examining the various versions of the poem, Góngora's attempt to prune away all traces of "learned" poetry in order to approximate his ballad as much as possible to the popular tradition.

It is not surprising, therefore, that "La más bella niña" was immensely popular in its own day and that, for nineteenth-century scholars who could not yet be affected by the rediscovery and reevaluation of Baroque poetry early in the present century, the ballad was a rare example of Góngora at his lucid best. The centrifuging of the Cordoban's poetry in terms of the aberrant longer works—and the shorter ballads and sonnets of the same ilk—that revealed his mental imbalance and the felicitous and charming shorter works that mirrored the best of the earlier balladry surrounded "La más bella niña" with an aura of praise not forthcoming for Góngora's literature as a whole. Although one can point to the definite use of rhetorical features—for example, of the synecdoche of the lover's eyes to refer to his whole person (if this is not actually a metonymy to allude to his sexuality)—they do not go beyond commonplace devices easily discoverable in the best of the supposedly unlearned and anonymous early ballads.

The text is divided into three segments: the opening *mise en scène* that introduces the girl's lament, the lament itself and the series of imperatives (erotesis) to her mother or to the night (lines 51, 55), and the second-person commands that make up the six complete refrains that end each of the six eight-line strophes. The refrain is grammatically ambiguous to the extent that each of the shores of the sea could be the subject of the verb (in which case the mother only hears the command given to the shores) or the plural verb form could be a polite command to the mother to allow the girl to cry *at* the shores of the sea (premodern Spanish, like modern French, could use a familiar plural to express a polite imperative to one person). The latter is usually taken to be the correct interpretation, although the former would have some justification in that we suppose the shores of the sea to have seen the embarkation of the beloved. Assuming, however, that the mother is the correct subject of the imperative, although the girl's own voice dominates as she speaks her emotional dirge, the mother is seen to be both her audience and the insistent backdrop of the occasion for the lament. And it is significant that the girl, despite her obvious attachment to him, does not once apostrophize the beloved. More on this below.

The five stanzas of the dirge itself show an asymmetrical pattern—the addition of two strophes has destroyed the symmetry of the three stanzas of the version popularized in the 1600 *Romancero nuevo.* Stanza one, for example, rather than being a straightforward complaint over the beloved's departure, appears more to be addressed to the mother as a justification for complaining to *her,* which is an alternative to aching alone in silence (or, in order that there be a poem in the girl's own voice, mourning alone in the bed which is now too big by half [cf. lines 57–58]). Stanzas two and four of the lament refer to the central action of weeping as indicative of the girl's grief, while stanza five of the lament is an indirect command to night to be gone since she is no longer able to enjoy it in the arms of her lover. (Stanza two also involves in passing an indirect command.) In stanza three of the lament, as in stanza one, the girl addresses her mother directly and again she appears interested in justifying to the older woman her right to express her new-found grief. Thus, there is a certain symmetry between the first four stanzas of the lament itself, which are in turn the central four stanzas of the six that make up the poem as a whole. The four strophes in question alternate addresses. In the last stanza, it is more as if the girl were simply speaking herself; the third-person indirect command has the effect of destroying the mood of one person reporting directly to a second person that characterizes the bulk of the composition.

What about the lament itself? Despite the carefully studied popular aura which Góngora was able to achieve with this composition, there are undeniable traces of what can only be called a learned rhetoric, not to mention evidence of some typically Baroque expressive devices. First of all, we can leave aside the reference to the eyes of the lover; we have already suggested that such a device is not completely audacious, and one can find similar synecdoches in the earliest courtly love poetry of the fifteenth-century *Cancioneros (Songbooks).* And in addition one has only to refer to the common cliché of Western love poetry that the eyes are the windows of the soul to understand the frequency of preoccupations with the eyes of the beloved in the poetry of the Renaissance. Much more striking in terms of typical poetic devices to be found in Góngora's supposed more labored and hermetic poetry is the formula to be found in lines 14–15. Dámaso Alonso has repeatedly shown that there is a series of expressive formulas preferred by the poet which essentially provide a double epithet of X by saying that X is A but not B, or that X is A if it is (at least) not B, or that X is now A, now B, and so on.[11]

When the girl tells her mother that the enthrallment in love which the mother has presumably caused the daughter has meant a pleasure which is short but a grief which is long, we have another but more complex manifestation of the same double-epithet formula. In this case X (that which the daughter has been given) is A (shortness of pleasure), as well as B (length of grief). What is important here is that in this formula, A and B are the obverse of each other, or are in an inversely proportional relationship. Thus, to use the common mathematical formulation, $A = 1/B$: shortness is (semantically) the inverse of length. In the ballad to be discussed below, the difficult text on Angélica and Medoro's pastoral idyll, lines 13 and 14 show the same formula: the man (X) has veins with little blood (A), but eyes with much sight (1/B). The meaning is that he has lost much blood and his eyes are glazed with shock, but the expression comes through a formula which plays on the inverse relationship between little and much. In this way, we can see how the apparently artless surface of "La más bella niña" reveals upon closer examination some of the same devices to be found in the most difficult of the poems.

Wardropper has pointed out for the third stanza what can only be called a laconic conceit. Here, the manner of describing the girl's having given herself over completely to tearful lamentations involves an ecphrasis, an explanation, of her emotions. Rather than simply commanding her eyes to be perpetually awash in tears out of grief, the girl explains that the sweet occupation of looking has been replaced by crying. Why this is effective poetically derives from the transference from one function of the eyes to another which is integrally related to the first. Thus, the eyes are to be converted from looking, which is indeed a sweet occupation when they have the beloved to gaze upon (cf. lines 25–28), to the secondary occupation of crying. Not only does the conceit express the movement from sweet looking to tearful sorrow, but—and this is important for an age which believed in the inherent nature of certain phenomena (natural theology) and which saw in the concept of Ovidian metamorphosis an allegory of the human circumstance (see Góngora's *Polifemo* discussed in Chapter 4)—it as well dwells on the disruption of what is natural (i.e., for the eyes to look) and the imposition of what is not (for the eyes to cry).

The conceit, then, coming as it does at the center of the composition, functions to imply the momentous nature of the girl's loss: so momentous is it for her that she would implore her eyes to metamorphose their inherent function as an expression of her emotional state. All of this may seem overly insistent for a poem which ostensibly tells quite simply of a girl crying her eyes out over the loss of her lover. But to miss the important function of the conceit in the third stanza is to overlook the manner in which the poet uses conceits, which on the surface may appear to be completely unostentatious, to express as strikingly and as laconically as possible the crux of the human emotion involved. Along the same lines, it is worth noting how further metaphors on eyes are expressed in the last stanza. Not only are two sets of eyes contrasted, his (line 53) and hers (line 54), but the association of the latter with the verb "stay awake" in line 54 and the use of the former, as previously in the poem, to refer synecdochally to the beloved, is tantamount to zeugma—what we have is a blend of the literal and the figurative. In addition, the indirect command to the night to be gone (line 51) is extended in line 55 for the night not to see the solitude in which the girl has been left. (The use of the word solitude here is charged with much more meaning for a Hispanic audience than it would be for an English-language one, since the theme of solitude in Hispanic poetry bespeaks a fundamental human circumstance; cf. the Portuguese *saudades*, so often expressed in the famous *fados.*[12]) In addition to the foregoing, there are a number of other rhetorical flourishes that bear brief mention: the antithesis between peace and war (lines 27–28), between good and bad (lines 35–36), the commonplaces of the prison of love (line 17), verdant youth (lines 46–48), and possibly another formula of inversion (lines 33–34).

One aspect of the ballad which has not received extensive discussion concerns the object of the girl's apostrophe. Why should the mother be forced to bear the burden of blame for the love affair (stanza two)? Unless we simply attribute the accusations to the general hysteria of the abandoned beloved, we cannot easily answer the question. We then must seek another explanation that justifies the language of the girl. The only other "mother" of a girl that comes readily to mind, particularly a desperate girl in love, is Venus.

While it is true that the goddess of love is usually invoked by men who have been treacherously attacked by her son, Cupid (Góngora has several ballads along these more traditional lines), this fact may be due more simply to the higher frequency of men as narrative voices in poetry than women, rather than to anything inappropriate about a woman addressing her sexual mentor. Diana is of course the protectress of women who would remain chaste in the face of the implorations of ardent suitors, but it is obvious that the girl of our ballad has already given herself over to the pleasures of physical love. Now that she is alone, abandoned, and considerably disturbed over the fleeting nature of these pleasures, it seems not at all strange that she should rail against the person under whose aegis women give rein to their sensuality.[13] From this point of view, the girl's harsh words to her "mother" are addressed, not to any biological love (see Garcilaso de la Vega's famous poem, "To the Flower of Cnidus," his "Canción V," in which he urges woman to abandon her cruel ways and perfect herself by pursuing her true role as a daughter of Venus). Venus, whose machinations few can resist, caused the girl to fall in love at such a tender age, Venus handed her over to the prison of love, whose gaolkeeper is the beloved now gone off to war, taking with him the keys to her heart. In short, Venus, the inspiration of the girl's love affair, now becomes the only likely object for the attacks of her despairing solitude and hysteria: the implication is that, as far as the girl is concerned, it would have been better for her not to have been given in love than now to experience personally the bitter truth of the formula expressed in lines 13–14.

From a purely intrinsic point of view, the interpretation of the mother of "La más bella niña" as necessarily the Venus mother-figure of all women in poetic love is impossible to "prove." But to want to see the mother as a Venus who has been the perpetrator of the love affair between girl and departed warrior, thereby fulfilling her time-honored role in Western mythology, is one way of calling attention to an integral function for the presence of the older woman. The girl's dirge is not spoken in a vacuum; hers is not simply an unfortunate solitude born of the casual vicissitudes of love. It is a solitude and a grief deriving from the very inherent, unstable nature of that paradigmatic human emotion, love. The addressing of the lament and its parallel accusations to a mother, a Venus, who is the embodiment of that emotion only serves to heighten any correlation between the girl's circumstance and the basic human condition that the poet most likely wished to suggest. The surface texture of the poem may be an exercise in studied artlessness, but its structure reveals unmistakably Góngora's concern in his more serious poetry with a vision of man's lot.

III *The Narrative Ballad*

The *Romance de Angélica y Medoro (Ballad of Angélica and Medoro),* agreed to be from 1602, is easily one of Góngora's most brilliant and widely-known compositions. Based on a passage from the Italian Ludovico Ariosto's influential sixteenth-century *Orlando furioso* (*Mad Roland;* a very loose reworking of traditional Roland materials), Góngora's ballad has received extensive attention as a standard anthology piece and from the critics as an example of the inextricable entwinement of aspects of "un-Baroque" clarity, particularly in the use of what had become a popular story and in its treatment within the traditional ballad genre, as well as of typical aspects of Baroque style and structure. Indeed, some of the first attempts to dispel the critical errors concerning a facile Góngora and a difficult, decadent—Baroque—Góngora focused on the *Ballad of Angélica and Medoro* in order to show the poetic force of the entwinement of the two threads.[14] The rest is critical history, with the result that the ballad is recognized to be a cornerstone not only of Góngora's poetry as a whole (as a ballad its popularity and diffusion are challenged only by the *romancillo* discussed above), but as well of the typical problems presented by the best of the poet's work. Language and historical backgrounds have been discussed at length by previous treatments; the following presentation will stress difficult questions of theme and unity of structure, with particular emphasis on the influence of traditional ballad format.[15] The text, while long, deserves extensive quoting:

	En un pastoral albergue	(In a pastoral shelter
	que la guerra entre unos robres	which the war, among some oaks,
	lo dejó por escondido	missed, because hidden,
	o lo perdonó por pobre,	or ignored, because poor,
5	*do la paz viste pellico*	where peace wears a skin jacket

y conduce entre pastores
ovejas del monte al llano

y cabras del llano al monte,

mal herido y bien curado
10 *se alberga un dichoso joven,*
que sin clavarle Amor flecha

le coronó de favores.
Las venas con poca sangre,
los ojos con mucha noche,
15 *lo halló en el campo aquella*
vida y muerte de los hombres.
Del palafrén se derriba,
no porque al moro conoce,
sino por ver que la hierba
20 *tanta sangre paga en flores.*
Límpiale el rostro, y la mano
siente al Amor que se esconde
tras las rosas, que la muerte
va violando sus colores.
25 *Escondióse tras las rosas*
porque labren sus arpones
el diamante del Catay
con aquella sangre noble.
. . . .
45 *Los últimos nudos daba*
cuando el cielo la socorre
de un villano en una yegua
que iba penetrando el bosque.
Enfrénanle de la bella
50 *las tristes piadosas voces,*
que los firmes troncos mueven
y las sordas piedras oyen;
y la que mejor se halla
en las selvas que en la Corte,
55 *simple bondad, al pío ruego*
cortésmente corresponde.

Humilde se apea el villano
y sobre la yegua pone
un cuerpo con poca sangre,
60 *pero con dos corazones;*

and leads, among shepherds,
sheep from the mountain to the plain
and goats from the plain to the mountain,
badly wounded and well cured,
there lodges a lucky youth
whom Love, without piercing him with arrows
crowned him with favors.
his veins with little blood,
his eyes with much night,
she found him in the fields who
is the life and death of men.
She dismounts from the palfrey,
not because she knows the Moor,
but because she sees the grass
pays for so much blood in flowers.
She cleans his face, and her hand
perceives Love who is hiding
behind the roses, for death
is doing violence to their colors.
He hid behind the roses
in order for his arrows to work
the diamond of Cathay
with that noble blood.
She was tying the last knots
when heaven helps her
in the form of a villager on a mare
who was passing through the forest.
The sad piteous cries of the
beautiful woman make him stop,
which move the stolid trunks
and which the deaf stones hear;
and that simple kindness that
is more easily found in the
forest than at Court
corteously responds to the pitiful plea.
The villager humbly dismounts
and on his mare places
a body with little blood,
but one with two hearts;

	a su cabaña los guía,	to his cabin he guides them,
	que el Sol deja su horizonte	while the sun is leaving its horizon
	y el humo de su cabaña	and the smoke from his cabin
	les va sirviendo de Norte.	serves as a North Star for them.
65	*Llegaron temprano a ella,*	They soon arrive there
	do una labradora acoge	where a farmer's wife takes in
	un mal vivo con dos almas,	a man barely alive with two souls
	y una ciega con dos soles.	and a blind woman with two suns.
	Blando heno en vez de pluma	Soft hay instead of feathers
70	*para lecho les compone,*	she uses for a bed for them,
	que será tálamo luego	one which will later be a bower
	do el garzón sus dichas logre	where the youth will achieve his delights.
	. . . .	
	Todo sirve a los amantes;	Everything serves the lovers;
110	*plumas les baten, veloces,*	swift feathers beat for them
	airecillos lisonjeros,	flattering breezes,
	si no son murmuradores.	if not ones that gossip.
	Los campos les dan alfombras,	The fields give them carpets,
	los árboles pabellones,	the trees pavilions,
115	*la apacible fuente sueño,*	the peaceful spring sleep,
	música los ruiseñores.	music the nightingales.
	Los troncos les dan cortezas	The trunks give them barks
	en que se guarden sus nombres	to store their names
	mejor que en tablas de mármol	better than on tablets of marble
120	*o que en láminas de bronce*	or on plates of brass.
	No hay verde fresno sin letra,	There is no green ash without a letter,
	ni blanco chopo sin mote;	no white poplar without an emblem;
	si un valle "Angélica" suena,	if one valley rings with "Angélica,"
	otro "Angélica" responde.	another answers back with "Angélica,"
125	*Cuevas do el silencio apenas*	Caves where silence hardly
	deja que sombras las moren	allows shadows to dwell
	profanan con sus abrazos	are profaned with their embraces,
	a pesar de sus horrores.	despite the caves' horrors.
	Choza, pues, tálamo y lecho,	Hut, then, wedding bower and bed,
130	*cortesanos labradores,*	courtly farmers,
	aires, campos, fuentes, vegas,	breezes, fields, springs, meadows,
	cuevas, troncos, aves, flores,	caves, trunks, birds, flowers,
	fresnos, chopos, montes, valles,	ash trees, poplars, mountains, valleys,
	contestes de estos amores,	witnesses of these loves,
135	*el cielo os guarde, si pueda,*	may heaven protect you, if it can,
	de las locuras del Conde.[16]	from the madness of the Count.)[17]

There are many striking features about this composition that coincide to provide the intense impact that it has had on most readers. Most obvious is the antithetical, virtually contradictory, juxtaposition of the encomium of pastoral life—the poem is in its entirety an elaboration of the Renaissance commonplace of the "praise of the countryside and the scorning of the court" (cf. lines 53–56, for one explicit example)—and the difficult artificial language in which the work is written, although the difficulty lies not so much in the vocabulary. The poem is not primarily *cultista,* although there are some traces of it, such as the famous example of Greek accusative which introduces the description of Angélica under the full sway of love in line 101; "Desnuda el pecho anda ella (she goes about bare of breast)," where the feminine adjective *(desnuda)* agrees, not with the masculine noun it modifies *(pecho),* but with the feminine referent of the latter (Angélica). This pseudo-Greek syntax for what standard Spanish would paraphrase, capturing the same agreement pattern, as "Ella anda desnuda de pecho." Indeed, along with a handful of language traits such as this instance of the Greek accusative, one finds also, and surprisingly, very colloquial, almost burlesque turns of phrase such as the phrase in 107, equivalent in tone to English "scram." The linguistic difficulty of the text, which is so deliberately counterpoised to the ostensible bucolic simplicity stressed by the actual content, is more semantic and has to do with the very density of allusive and metaphoric meaning of key stanzas.

It is appropriate that language, the very medium of poetry, be the most significant characteristic of the ballad. In addition, several thematic features contribute to the singular nature of the work: the interplay between "real" war and the commonplaces of the "war of love"; the martial figure of Orlando, never actually present, but always felt behind every moment of the poem, vs. the figure of idyllic Cupid; the figure of the transitory Vale of Tears that is man's mortal lot and the figure of the lost Garden of Eden, which the latter-day Adam and Eve attempt in vain to recover through their love; the antonomastic contrast between the Angélica-Diana before her discovery of Medoro and the Angélica-Venus of their ensuing bliss; and, finally, the backdrop of harmonious, perfect Nature that man may be "pure" enough to partake of and to enhance mutually (Angélica and Medoro) or that he, more likely, will be inclined to corrupt (Orlando).

The ballad is divided into two roughly equal movements. Lines 1–72 describe the meeting of these two prototypic figures of human beauty; lines 73–136 describe the relationship that develops between them, a relationship that bespeaks, albeit fleetingly, what was to have been the perfect love of the primeval couple in absolute harmony with Nature. To this extent, Góngora goes beyond the commonplace evocation of a pastoral setting, as one perceives from the initial verse, to stress the very real relationship between such a setting and the archetypal Garden of Eden which underlies man's recurring sense of original sin and imperfection. While it might be argued that such a relationship obtains in all pastoral or idyllic literature, particularly that of the Renaissance,[18] we are not here relying on a hypothetical mythic interpretation, "necessary because universal," but rather on explicit references within the text that will be discussed in detail.

Adhering to the most typical aspect of the traditional anonymous ballads, *Angélica and Medoro* begins in *medias res* with the information that Medoro has been sidelined on the field of battle, fallen wounded in some shepherd's shelter that had been spared the destruction of war. It is customary to assume that Góngora's contemporary readers must have recognized immediately the well-known references to passages of Ariosto's poem and filled in from that recognition the background concerning both Medoro, the Moor, and Angélica, the beautiful but disdainful Princess of Cathay, who is pursued heatedly but with comic failure by the crazed Count Orlando (Roland of the Charlemagne stories, but here wildly distorted to suit the Italian's bitingly ironic vision of martial and courtly ideals). As in the case of the early ballads also, the abrupt conclusion of the text was probably less cryptic to a seventeenth-century reader, who would have realized immediately the Count referred to his threat to devastate all that opposed his conquest of the ever-elusive Angélica, and, quite extrinsic to Góngora's text, the escape from him of the lovers to Cathay to live, one assumes, happily everafter. Normally the modern reader cannot be expected to grasp the periphrastic allusions to persons and events without some textual assistance. Indeed, one might justify the use of periphrasis, as part of the attempt precisely to avoid explicit reference via what was already too well known. Thus, for example, rather than identifying Angélica by name and referring to the devastating affect wrought upon men's souls by both her beauty and her cold disdain, the poet first refers to the woman as "that life and death of men" (lines 15–16), and then speaks of love marshalling his harpoons "to work with that noble blood [Medoro's] the diamond of Cathay" (lines 26–28). The latter is significant not only for its use of the lost popular belief that only blood can soften diamonds, but for the assumption that we will know that the "diamond of Cathay" is Angélica and, more important, that Love's attack is spectacular precisely because Angélica has up until now been successful in protecting herself from Cupid's darts. Moreover, in a doubling of the irony, we are informed that it is she, and not Medoro, unlike other men, who falls in love first (lines 11–12). The density of references here, making identification of principals and isolation of exact circumstance tricky, is increased by the covert mention in lines 11–12 of Angélica—whom Love will have cured but not made to fall in love—who has yet even to appear on the scene. The double thrust of these observations is that they both recall the often cryptic introit of the traditional ballads, a characteristic usually attributed to their origin through fragmentation of the longer epic compositions, but also the hermetic, impenetrable meaning associated with the epitome of Baroque expression.

This introduction of the two protagonists, the pastoral setting of their encounter, which interrupts one of Angélica's many flights from the mad Count (cf. lines 17 ff.), and the dramatic effect upon the woman by the physically wounded man, with whom she falls irretrievably in love, figuratively wounded herself by the darts of Love hidden within his moribund cheeks (cf. lines 21 ff.), includes a crucial reference to the setting as a figure of the Garden of Eden. The lines that describe Angélica as struck by the darts of Love hidden in the roses that are Medoro's cheeks are a conceitful accommodation of the "serpent in the grass" that is metaphoric of man's original sin. But whereas in the original and worn biblical myth, the serpent effects his betrayal of man hidden among the forbidden fruit of power (i.e., the apple by popular tradition), here the evil serpent has become the sweet Love who works his design from among the roses that are symbolic in Western tradition of sensual and youthful love (cf. the saying "gather ye rosebuds while ye may," treated by Góngora in the sonnet discussed below pp. 63ff.). On one level it is beside the point that the roses referred to are in turn periphrastic symbols of Medoro's cheeks and, more generally, of his overpowering beauty. That the reference to roses can function on two separate levels of meaning, to refer both to the man as well as to the significance of Love's labor wrought within a specific context, bespeaks the sort of laconic style, to use Dámaso Alonso's description, that characterizes Góngora's verbal art. Thus, Angélica's hand is "bit" by Love as she applies her Oriental arts of surgery to the wounded man. Buι it is significant that the wound she receives is not the correlative to sin, as in the case of Eve (and note that like Eve, it is Angélica who takes the initiative, who leads Medoro in their awakening to Love), but rather of pure love, an emotion which she experiences supposedly for the first time and which will define the limits of her most perfect realization as a human being.

This allusion to the pastoral setting as a figure of Eden is borne out by the superficially facile but structurally crucial reference in lines 53–56 to the conflict between country and court. When the peasant who hears the woman's piteous appeals for help comes to her aid, he is described as manifesting that simple goodness which is more to be found in the country than at court, a sentiment which is such a commonplace of Western literature as to merit almost no further attention if it were not directly related to the basic tone of the poem toward the encounter between Angélica and Medoro. Here we have two individuals who are recognized to be epitomes of the perfect courtiers. And even if we cannot affirm that Medoro's involvement in the war which casts him into the shepherd's shelter at the outset of the composition is adequate internal evidence of his courtly position, the references to Angélica's royal station and her amorous pursuit by men establish concretely her own identification with what modern man would call the dehumanization of the court. But it is precisely that complex of nonbucolic customs that has brought the two together—he because of the war, and she because of the warrior from whom she is forced to flee. Orlando, of course, embodies a fusion of the two warlike aspects of the court, for he is known as the mightiest military arm of Charlemagne as well as the most prodigious participant in the courtly war of love between the sexes, as Angélica well knows in her perpetual flight before his insistent siege of her person. Thus, the reproachful ways of the court bring the two together, but circumstance, the ideal beauty of Medoro, and, most important, Love's swift labor in the archetypal setting, combine to bring out in Angélica a fateful charity, Christian or otherwise. This charity is the "simple goodness" to which the poet refers after the fact, when Angélica can no longer retrace the steps which brought her to Medoro and her attention to his wounds. Her charity, either rewarded or reinforced by the white fire of pure emotion that Love for once (and for all) accords her, is the basis of the first segment of the ballad, which concludes with a summary of the perfect cure that Medoro enjoys at her hands.

The second segment of the poem is given over to an evocation of the ideal love that is born between them. There are two crucial aspects of the figurative recovery of the Garden of Eden presented in this last half of the ballad. One is a more explicit affirmation of the positive powers of Love. The poet speaks of love making his bowstring, the instrument of Angélica's first emotion, into a whip to drive Envy from the idyllic setting (lines 85–92). Here Envy fulfills a double function. On one level, she is the personification of an aspect of courtly existence and as such is inappropriate to the pastoral ideal of the present circumstance. (And note that in lines 99–100, in their pastoral setting, they have even made perfect Venus' courtly war of love.) Her exile is the banishment of any last symbolic vestige of a way of life that would impede the development of the intense relationship between the two lovers. On another level, one can see Envy as the anti-figure of Love. If Love is the highest virtue of this pair, then Envy, which Love belabors with his bowstring-whip, is the lowest vice. Like the serpent of Eden, traditionally described as envious of man's original favored place before God, Envy must be banished from this idyll if the recovery of the intense happiness of the primeval Garden is to be complete. But the poet assigns to this passage an even higher role. For all major commentaries on the poem, these two stanzas are simply a brilliant ecphrasis of the level of ecstasy achieved by the pair, watched over and protected by the Guardian Angel of Love responsible for their ideal passion.

Nevertheless, in order to understand fully the importance of this passage, it must be compared with the closing couplet, the other major aspect of the poem—indeed, lines 135–36 provide an overall tone for our understanding of the entire composition. Here, we must second E. M. Wilson's assessment of the poem, that "*Angélica and Medoro* expresses the intensity and precariousness of human happiness."[19] That is to say, the ballad concludes with a typical note of Baroque disillusionment and preoccupation with the transitory nature of all human experience, happiness above all. It is important to gauge how this concluding note is presented. The poet has devoted twenty-six verses to describing the perfect harmony between the lovers and Nature—every element of nature contributes to and collaborates with their passion, and the last six lines preceding the concluding couplet are an impressive accumulation of no fewer than sixteen nouns that refer to this harmony. In the final 1602 text of the ballad, Góngora added this accumulation to his earlier version, thus strengthening the shock of transition between the "leisurely" buildup of detail concerning the lovers' state of bliss and the abrupt two-line return to the inescapable reality of human existence. What we are left with, then, is the implication that all of this is transitory, that the two will be returned to the cruel circumstances that preceded their encounter, courtly war and courtly amorous pursuit by an enraged and crazed Orlando. The effect is to destroy whatever atmosphere of nobility of spirit, ideal human experience, etc., that is achieved by the main body of the ballad. Góngora's implication is obvious: man may come accidently to possess the ingredients of a return to the primeval innocence and purity of soul of the Garden of Eden, but he should not be deceived by such opportunities, for the forces of evil, of sheer human experience, doom him inescapably to spiritual and physical destruction.

In this sense, the "charming" banishment of Envy by Love is but incidental, marginal to the true circumstance of the transitory event. Love may banish Envy, may collaborate temporarily in the realization of that perfect harmony and union of the lovers and nature, but he will obviously be impotent in the face of the most fundamental challenge to that harmony and unity: reality itself. Because of this sense of the last segment of the stanza, the intense irony surrounding the description of edenic passion, one must disagree strongly with R. O. Jones's essentially extrinsic reading of the poem.[20] Basing himself on the reasonable argument that Góngora's audience can be expected to have known the outlines of the story according to Ariosto, he arrives at the highly unreasonable conclusion that, because the lovers manage to escape Orlando's wrath in the Italian's narrative poem, we should assume that this is also the case with the Spaniard's ballad—thus, the latter has a "happy ending."

This is unacceptable, since not only is it a reading arrived at on the basis of Ariosto's poem and not Góngora's, but it also misses the entire sense of the ballad. As we have shown, the ballad strives to create a figure of Eden toward which the two lovers grope, only to have it overcast by the imminent doom of Orlando's fury. This is, of course, almost so archetypically Baroque, so reminiscent of the somber pessimism vis-à-vis human existence to be found in the sonnets, as to be not worth emphasizing—it is precisely what we expect to find. Moreover, as has been shown, the structure of the ballad, the ironic foreshadowing assumed by the role of Love, the importance of the juxtaposition of the final accumulation of collaborating elements of Nature and the abrupt concluding couplet that breaks the entire foregoing mood, justify the more pessimistic interpretation of the last two lines and also reinforce its overall importance for grasping the larger irony of the sure doom which must befall man's terrestrial gropings after the Garden of Eden.

IV *An Example of Narrative Structuring*

	Servía en Orán al Rey	(There served the King in Orán
	un español con dos lanzas,	a Spaniard with two lances,
	y con el alma y la vida	and with his soul and life
	a una gallarda africana,	he served a graceful African maiden,
5	*tan noble como hermosa,*	as noble as she was beautiful,
	tan amante como amada,	as loving as she was loved,
	con quien estaba una noche	with whom he was one night
	cuando tocaron al arma.	when the call to arms was sounded.
	Trescientos cenetes eran	Three hundred warriors of Zeneta
10	*de este rebato la causa,*	were the cause of this alarm,
	que los rayos de la luna	and the moon's rays
	descubrieron sus adargas;	revealed their leather shields;
	las adargas avisaron	the shields warned
	a las mudas atalayas,	the silent watchtowers,
15	*las atalayas los fuegos,*	the watchtowers the fires,
	los fuegos a las campanas;	the fires the bells;
	y ellas al enamorado,	and the latter the lover
	que en los brazos de su dama	who in the arms of his lady
	oyó el militar estruendo	heard the military uproar
20	*de las trompas y las cajas.*	of the trumpets and the drums.
	Espuelas de honor le pican	Spurs of honor jab him
	y freno de amor le para;	and love's bit reins him;

	no salir es cobardía,	not to go is cowardliness,
	ingratitud es dejalla.	to leave her is ingratitude.
25	*Del cuello pendiente ella,*	Hanging around his neck,
	viéndole tomar la espada,	seeing him take up the sword,
	con lágrimas y suspiros	with tears and sighs
	le dice aquestas palabras:	she speaks these words to him:
	«Salid al campo señor,	"Be off to the field, sir:
30	*bañen mis ojos la cama;*	let my eyes bathe the bed,
	que ella me será también,	for without you it will be
	sin vos, campo de batalla.	for me also a battlefield.
	»Vestíos y salid apriesa,	Dress and hurry away,
	que el general os aguarda;	for the general awaits you:
35	*yo os hago a vos mucha sobra*	you no longer need me
	y vos a él mucha falta.	and he needs you greatly.
	»Bien podéis salir desnudo,	Well might you go forth naked,
	pues mi llanto no os ablanda;	since not even my tears can touch you
	que tenéis de acero el pecho	your heart is of steel
40	*y no habéis menester armas.»*	and you have no need of arms."
	Viendo el español brioso	The determined Spaniard, seeing
	cuánto le detiene y habla,	how she detains him and how she
	le dice así: «Mi señora,	speaks, says thus to her: "My lady
	tan dulce como enojada,	as sweet as you are angry,
45	*porque con honra y amor*	in order that I may with honor
	yo me quede, cumpla y vaya,	and with love remain, comply, and go,
	vaya a los moros el cuerpo	let my body go to the Moors
	y quede con vos el alma.	and my soul remain with you.
	Concededme, dueño mío,	Grant me, my mistress,
50	*licencia para que salga*	license to go forth
	al rebato en vuestro nombre	to the attack in your name
	y en vuestro nombre combata.»[21]	and in your name do battle.")[22]

The preceding composition belongs to an important subgenre of the Spanish ballad in the Renaissance called the "Moorish, artistic ballad." These poems may sentimentalize the Moorish culture—as will the Byzantine literature of Romanticism—or, as is the case with Góngora's early poem—may, with a controlled interest in the exotic, simply find in that context a universal conflict in accord with the interests of the general Western tradition. In the case of this ballad, the conflict is the heady one between the obligations of military service and those of amorous service, the latter, within the convention of courtly love (which may or may not have been inspired by

Arabic sources and traditions via Southern France), every bit as demanding and stringent as the former. What is particularly Moorish, of course, is the general setting: the somewhat unusual circumstance of a valiant Spaniard ("with two lances") who serves a pagan king during the last days of the Reconquest (Orán fell to the Spanish in 1509) and the definitely exotic note of the love between the Christian knight and the African (Moorish) maiden. Although the theme of such an amorous relationship is quite frequent in the literature of the period—and indeed this ballad appears to have some lesser literary antecedents[23]—it continued to constitute enough of a note of the uncommon to function as the narrative core of ballads such as this one.

Despite the apparent thematic and expository simplicity of Góngora's ballad—the knight's being surprised by the call to arms while in his lover's arms, the conflict between equally weighty obligations, the ingenious resolution which is yet almost a cliché—the composition reveals not only the sort of stylistic features typically associated with Góngora in vocabulary and rhetoric; there is as well a considerable elaboration of a central structural motif that ties together the conflict between arms and love that can be called the point of the poem. We might speak of three dominant movements: the first two quatrains, which establish both narrative context as well as the central conflict that will flow from the unusual circumstance; the next four quatrains, which describe the unfortunate event that, coming as a wholly external and trivial catalyst, much in the fashion of the unfortunate machinations of Fortune which beleaguer the Renaissance skeptic, bringing to a flash point the conflict between the two contending obligations of love and arms; and, finally, the last seven quatrains, which constitute an example of dialogism in the exchange between the two lovers, she bespeaking the claims of love; he, the claims of arms while putting forth a resolution for that potentially tragic conflict. It is significant to note that each of the three movements highlights the central conflict. In the first movement, it is stated in the opening stanza. In the second movement, it is the last of the four quatrains, thereby underscoring both the untimeliness of the alarm as well as foreshadowing the exchange between the two lovers that concludes the ballad. And in the third movement, that conflict, aside from standing out by implication in the final words of the warrior, pervades the remarks of the narrator, the maiden and her lover, as we will demonstrate in detail below.

It is important to note the traditional characteristics of Góngora's ballad: the opening in *medias res,* the rapid movement to an inciteful situation that will bring into intense play a fundamental drama—usually concerning the feudal ethos in the early ballad, although situations of love and the human dilemma in general are quite frequently to be found—the dialogism by which the (pseudo-) minstrel increases the effect of immediacy of narration by allowing the principals of his momentary evocation of a vital conflict to utter their own intense reactions of the moment, and the abrupt conclusion that leaves final resolution of tension to the imagination of the audience. It is typical of the traditional Spanish ballad, for example, that we are not told the woman's reaction to her lover's inspired solution for his quandary, nor are we told anything else concerning the battle or the amorous relationship. In short, there is no follow-through of the narrative proper, and the result is the concentration of our attention on the nature of the conflict itself: the narrative *per se* becomes inconsequential and the conflict, only by virtue of skimpy personalization through two individuals who are allowed to speak, is barely prevented from being the sort of emotional abstraction associated with the tradition of the Petrarchan sonnet. On the other hand, a minute stylistic analysis of the poem would reveal a number of the Mannerist characteristics associated with Góngora's more complex poetry—and his ballads are often more pronounced in their use of these devices precisely because they are meant to be artificially popular in the external trappings of their genre. One notes, for example, the use of the metonymy in line two to describe the valor of the knight, although, as we shall argue, the "two" lances are necessary for structural unity. Lines 12–17 constitute a gradated anadiplosis that leads up to the climax of the sudden awakening of the lover to face the conflict with which circumstance has presented him. Anadiplosis is the beginning of successive lines or phrases by the final element of the preceding line or phrase; here it is used to describe a fateful chain reaction that culminates very effectively in the aforementioned literal as well as metaphoric awakening of the knight. Lines 21–22 and 23–24 also reveal the typical device of antithesis, here used to highlight once again the dilemma at issue; as we have noted, this stanza both concludes the presentation of the background of the conflict and prefigures the nature of the ensuing dramatic exchange between the two lovers, and we can thus ascribe to Góngora's rhetoric much more than a merely circumstantial decorative function.

We have spoken of the presence of a structural motif that gives unity to a narrative that can hardly be said to be firmly self-contained. At the same time, such a structural motif and its careful elaboration throughout the ballad provide the "artistic" justification of the composition to the degree that artistry rather than thematics is the primary function of literature. The central conflict, to which we have referred with some emphasis simply because it does constitute the insistent point of departure for virtually every phrase of the poem, is first suggested in the opening stanza. Although we are not from the outset entirely aware of the meaning of the double characterization of the Spaniard, we soon see that it is precisely what is going to provide the dramatic point of contention that is the mainstay of the Hispanic ballad. The warrior is described as, on the one hand, serving the King of Orán with *two* lances, which correlate with the *two* qualities—soul and life—with which in another quarter he serves the African maiden. It is important that there be such a bimembrational balance: not only arms vs. love, but an equal quality of arms vs. an equal quality of love. True human conflict can arise most effectively where the competing issues are of equal moral stature, as we are most assuredly meant to assume is the case with the service of love and the service of arms. Thus, we can characterize the public obligation—arms—as A and the private obligation—love—as B. Such a formalization of the two is necessary in order to detail effectively the elaboration of the structural motif.

The motif does not occur again until lines 21 ff. This is worth noting, for, on the one hand, the overt statement of a conflict between A and B is held back until after the climactic effect of the lamentable catalytic event and its verbal representation via anadiplosis, but also the poet allows himself the space necessary to dwell on the external circumstance that is, precisely, to bring out the quandary of the warrior's double service. When the ballad does return to the conflict in the sixth quatrain, it is significantly in terms of the aforementioned antithesis. In reality there are two antitheses that bespeak the man's all-too-present dilemma: the spurs of honor (A) vs. the bit of love (B)—and note that now not only do we have a concrete statement that a tension is indeed involved, but that in addition it is expressed in terms of physical torment—and cowardliness (A) vs. ingratitude (B). Thus, the direct enunciation of the problem is expressed negatively, once in terms of contending emotions (lines 21–22, the first antithesis) and once in terms of moral choices (lines 23–24, the second antithesis). Once this juxtaposition has been securely advanced, the poet pursues it with insistence through six additional reiterations, one somewhat complex, for a total of nine articulations in all, if we count the opening stanza.

Indeed, the content of the lovers' exchange diminishes considerably in importance once we realize that the poet's dominant concern is in the elaboration of his structural motif. Thus, in lines 25–26, she hangs from his neck (B) while, we are to assume, he hangs his sword from his side (A); in lines 30–32, she bemoans that her tear-stained bed (B), the scene of their unconcerned love but moments before, will become like the field of battle to which he must repair (A); likewise, now somewhat petulant, she tells him to be off, for she is now a burden to him (B), while the King must now need him so (A); or, again a bit unreasonably, she infers that since her tears, the "weapon" of her love, have not harmed him (B), he will need no armor against the weapons of war (A). Note that these four reiterations, all rather uncomplicated in their elaboration on the lips of the maiden of the conflict which has arisen, represent an inversion of terms. In the first three instances, and in consonance with the primacy given by the opening line to service to the King of Orán, mention of arms (A) precedes mention of love (B). Now that the conflict has become personalized in the words of the lovers, private love, which is threatened by public arms, is given first reference. But the implication is unquestionably "*this* that we have is to be destroyed by *that* from without." That the *that* is military battle only ironically increases the aura of threatened destruction voiced by the girl.

The eighth reiteration of the motif is complex, both in the embodiment in a hypothetical sentence (thus subjunctive rather than indicative verbs) and in its intrinsic formulation. The man is now speaking and he is about to propose a resolution to the disconcerting conflict which has arisen, "so that," he says, "with honor and love/remain (B), comply and [i.e., as well as] go [to battle]" (A). The variation in the pattern of reiteration is not in the conflict or in the order of presentation (B before A), but in the separation of "remain" (B) and "go" (A) by the verb "comply," which refers to *both* A and B, since what is definitely at issue is which obligation is to be chosen. Both involve obligation, compliance, and the man is about to propose a solution so that the verb "comply" will, in fact rather than in conflict, apply to both of the two services which he has assumed as a man of honor. Line 45 presents somewhat of a problem. Is the man to stay only out of love as opposed to going because of (knightly) honor? Certainly the latter is a more inviting interpretation symmetrically. Thus, the pattern would be: "honor" (A_1)/"love" (B_1) /"go" (A_2). The two poles are thus split between a focal verb and a modifying emotion, and, although in the case of the latter A precedes B, the result is an effective chiasmus, another rhetorical device frequently deployed by Góngora to increase the complexity of an image or metaphor.

Seen in these terms, the penultimate reiteration of the poem's structural motif is considerably more complex than the rest. Occupying, as it does, the next to the last position—potentially an emphatic one—it serves to provide a final insistent summary of the conflict before it is "dissipated" by the man's final words of resolution. The resolution is that the man must go forth to meet the Moors in body (A) while remaining with the woman in soul (B). Although this may be somewhat of a cliché, it does, almost in the Platonic terms of the rift between ideal and material, reduce the conflict of obligations to contending demands assignable to different "spheres" of his person. Therefore, no problem need exist at all, and supposedly the beloved is left satisfied with the knowledge of spiritual allegiance in place of the warm body which moments before lay beside her. Whether we are to imagine the woman satisfied or not is a speculative matter; what has happened is that the poem has gone full circle to return, via the lover's supposed resolution of the conflict, to the primacy of arms, as A precedes B, and thus he requests in the last quatrain her permission, like a good liege of love, to do battle in her name. The external, public demand on his person has submerged the personal and private demand on his love, the secondary service assumed by the Spanish knight. It is a service which, given the precarious nature of man's private, inner experiences as seen in the two preceding ballads that we have discussed, must yield to the circumstances imposed by unseeing fate. That the man's proposed resolution is meant to be taken as a weak and pale "justification," a self-delusion, of his yielding to the obligations of arms over the obligations of love perhaps explains why it is left open and without any satisfactory follow-up in terms of supposed subsequent events.

The overall effect, then, becomes one of individuals who must face as best they can the uncontrollable demands placed upon their inner beings. The proposed resolution and strikingly insistent buildup of irresolvable conflict is unsatisfactory precisely to the degree to which the resolution of human ethico-moral conflict is imposed, not by man himself, but by circumstance beyond his control. In terms of the artistry of a ballad which is deceptively facile on the surface, a structural motif is elaborated with a tangible insistence, so that it becomes an example of one of the ways in which art objectifies itself, only in order to bespeak the fragile and tenuous nature of the service of love which Western tradition has believed to be the most noble commitment of man. The Moorish maiden's petulance, aside from the conflict which it is made to bespeak, becomes, like the lament of the "prettiest girl," a frustrated recognition of the inevitable—the true Baroque disillusionment of Góngora's poetry.

V *The Ballad and Interior Duplication*

The last ballad which is to be treated in detail was composed on the eve, so to speak, of Góngora's major poems, the *Polyphemus* and the *Solitudes*, and, like them, also treats of universal themes expressed in terms of nature. Unquestionably, along with "La más bella niña," this is one of Góngora's most quoted ballads:

	En los pinares de Xúcar	(In the pinewoods of Júcar
	vi bailar unas serranas,	I saw some highland girls dancing,
	al son del agua en las piedras	to the sound of the water on the stones
	y al son del viento en las ramas.	and the sound of the wind in the branches.
5	*No es blanco coro de ninfas*	This is no white band of nymphs
	de las que aposenta el agua	such as lodge in the water,
	o las que venera el bosque,	or such as the woods worship,
	seguidoras de Dïana:	followers of Diana:
	serranas eran de Cuenca,	they are country girls from Cuenca,
10	*honor de aquella montaña,*	an honour to that hill,

	cuyo pie besan dos ríos	whose foot two rivers kiss
	por besar de ellas las plantas.	in order to kiss the soles of their feet.
	Alegres corros tejían	They were weaving happy dances,
	dándose las manos blancas	giving one another their white hands
15	*de amistad, quizá temiendo*	in friendship, perhaps in fear
	no la truequen las mudanzas.	that the changes in the dance might alter it . . .
	¡Qué bien bailan las serranas!	How well the highland girls dance!
	¡Que bien bailan!	How well they dance!
	El cabello en crespos nudos	Their hair in crisp curls
20	*luz da al Sol, oro a la Arabia,*	gives light to the sun, and gold to Arabia,
	cuál de flores impedido,	some have it bound with flowers,
	cuál de cordones de plata.	others in silver cords.
	Del color visten de el cielo,	They wear country cloth, of the colour of the sky
	si no son de la esperanza,	if not of hope,
25	*palmillas que menosprecian*	(cloth) that eclipses
	al zafiro y la esmeralda.	the sapphire and the emerald.
	El pie (cuando lo permite	Their feet, when the pin of their skirt allows,
	la brújula de la falda)	
	lazos calza, y mirar deja	wear thongs and reveal
30	*pedazos de nieve y nácar.*	pieces of snow and mother-of-pearl.
	Ellas, cuyo movimiento	Those girls who in their movements
	honestamente levanta	so modestly lift
	el cristal de la columna	the crystal of the column
	sobre la pequeña basa.	of its small base—
35	*¡Qué bien bailan las serranas!*	How well they dance, the highland girls!
	¡Qué bien bailan!	How well they dance!
	Una entre los blancos dedos	One bruising black strones (castanets)
	hiriendo negras pizarras,	between her ivory fingers,
	instrumento de marfil	an ivory instrument
40	*que las musas le invidiaran,*	that the Muses would envy,
	las aves enmudeció,	silenced the birds
	y enfrenó el curso del agua;	and checked the flow of the water;
	no se movieron las hojas,	the leaves did not stir,
	por no impedir lo que canta:	so as not to interrupt what she sings:
45	*«Serranas de Cuenca*	"The highland girls of Cuenca
	iban al pinar,	went to the pinewood,
	unas por piñones,	some for pine-cones,
	otras por bailar.	others to dance.
	Bailando y partiendo	The pretty highland-girls,

50	*las serranas bellas*	dancing and sharing
	un piñón con otro,	pine-cones with one another [?, breaking them against each other]
	si ya no es con perlas,	if not with the pearls (of their fingers),
	de amor las saetas	rejoice in exchanging
	huelgan de trocar,	the arrows of Cupid,
55	*unas por piñones*	some for pine-cones,
	otras por bailar.	others for a dance.
	Entre rama y rama,	Between branch and branch,
	cuando el ciego Dios	when the blind god
	pide al sol los ojos	begs the sun for eyes
60	*por verlas mejor,*	to see them better,
	los ojos del Sol	you will see them treading on the
	las veréis pisar,	eyes of the sun [i.e., the patches of sunlight beneath the trees],
	unas por piñones,	some for pine-cones,
	otras por bailar.»[24]	others for a dance.")[25]

Like the ballads discussed previously in this chapter, this composition is ostensibly based on an older, "folkloric" form of poetry, and, again Góngora's elaboration of his poem results in an eminently Baroque artifice with little relationship to the original genre. In this case, the original genre is what has been called the *poesía de tipo tradicional* (poetry of a traditional sort),[26] which means the early miscellaneous, popular, and quasi-popular forms of lyric expression to be found in the Spanish dialects.

Despite the lack of formal stanzaic divisions, the present ballad may be seen in terms of two movements: the narrator's introduction, focusing on the personal *vi* (I saw) of line 2 (lines 1–36), and the reporting of the song of one of the girls (lines 37–64). In turn, the first part may be subdivided into the statement of setting (lines 1–18) and the purely decorative, hyperbolic description of the shepherdesses (lines 19–36). These two divisions are marked by the first refrain mentioned above; each one of these two initial subdivisions closes with a statement of this refrain (lines 17–18 and 35–36). The second movement of the poem may also be subdivided into the narrator's observation of the singer (lines 37–44) and the direct quote of the song itself (lines 45–64). One could call it typical of the ballad that the composition concludes with the song, without any return to the narrator's point of view—that is to say, there is no final commentary that brings us back to the initial point of departure of the text. This lack of the developmental symmetry associated with some forms of lyrical poetry, quite often in the form of refrains that are deployed throughout the poem, as in the case of much of the poetry of the fifteenth-century Spanish *Cancioneros (Songbooks),* is adopted by Góngora from the ballads, as we have noted in the previous ballad. Although the two movements themselves and their subdivisions are not symmetrical in any sense—there is no overt formal correlation between them, although the two subdivisions of the first movement are an even split between the first thirty-six lines—that there are progressive divisions within the poem that mark shifts in focus is less indicative of the traditional ballad than it is of formal Renaissance poetry such as the sonnet.

As a lyric composition, "En los pinares de Xúcar" is more completely decorative than narrative or even personally subjective. That is to say, although there is the tangible presence of the poetic voice within the composition, there is no real focus on that voice as such, as we have, for example, in the vast majority of the Renaissance sonnets. The narrator is simply an incidental witness to a scene, a tableau. Although a song is sung, and thus one must assume that it is a "true" scene of pastoral nature, it is as though he were observing an exquisitely wrought Arcadian painting, where the backdrop of bucolic nature is but a flimsy pretense for the artist's spectacular decorative talents with his subjects.

Indeed, and without wanting to fall into trite comments on the metaphysics or ontology of poetry, we might say that part of the nature of the composition as Baroque artifice is the juxtaposition—tension, if you will—between the framework of verisimilitude (the artist's reportorial voice concerning what he has seen) and the idealized and purely decorative nature of both setting and song, as well as of the language used to describe the former and to express the latter. Although the Western tradition of bucolic poetry is based on such a juxtaposition, there does tend to be a direct correlation between such a characteristic and a putative Baroque desire to "counter" nature itself with the objective artifice of the poem.[27] This is certainly the path that Góngora will take in the complex elaborations of the major poems studied in Chapters 4 and 5.

Once we acknowledge the basically decorative nature of the composition, we are more easily able to understand its structure and to see its fundamental contrast with the more narratively expository structure of the other ballads discussed in this chapter (although "La más bella niña" does verge on being more of a "situation" poem than a narrative, and passages of *Angélica and Medoro* threaten to lose sight of the individual stories involved). In this sense, one cannot speak of any "theme" or "narrative matter" for "En los pinares de Xúcar," and the text is best seen as the opportunity for the poet to elaborate a series of decorative hyperboles to describe the setting, the shepherdesses, and their song. Again, it is the framework of a visual contemplation.

This is most true of the major structural characteristic of the composition, the best internal example of the implicit adherence to objective artifice. This characteristic is the interior duplication of the pastoral description itself, a duplication which is the basis of the relationship between the two movements of the poem that we have identified.[28] That is to say, in the first part or movement of the poem, we have a narrative voice—incidental, trivial, nonpersonal, perhaps, but nevertheless there, giving the poem a flimsy identification with external reality. This narrative voice identifies the setting and proceeds to describe the shepherd girls who are disporting themselves in an apparently complete abandonment to simple pleasures of work and dance. If the poem concluded with the second occurrence of the first refrain in line 36, it would be a rather conventional and brief pastoral description. But the poet proceeds in a second movement to describe the song of one of the girls. That song is essentially a reelaboration of the narrator's own initial description. While the images don't necessarily match in the two movements, more important, tone and language do. Therefore, while it is not startling for the narrator to indulge in hyperboles of description in lines 20 (the girls' hair is so dazzling that it gives light to the sun and gold to Arabia) and 30–33 (the girls' feet are snow and mother-of-pearl and their legs are crystal columns), etc., that the song of one of those same girls, rustic maidens, indulges in the same sort of imagery is a violent and significant refutation of even a superficial verisimilitude that stresses the creation of an objective poetic artifice that will, as we have stated, counter nature itself.

Thus, the song also contains impressive hyperboles, such as the statement in lines 49–54, which are none too easy to grasp at a first reading, that the others are dancing and breaking open pinions, some by striking two together, some by using their pearls (that is, their teeth—this is the same sort of imagery as the narrator uses in lines 30–33), while all along wishing to exchange their rustic tasks for the arrows of Love. These few lines reveal much about what Góngora's poem does in terms of interior duplication. There is the use of a variant in lines 51–52 of the "A, B" formula, which the reader should by now see as perhaps the most fundamental Baroque rhetorical device to be found in Góngora's poetry: if they don't break the pinions by striking two together (A), then they do it with their teeth (B). The narrator had already also used such a formula in his description of their clothing in lines 23–26: if their clothing is not as blue as the sky, such as to scorn the sapphire (A), then it is as green as the color of hope, such as to scorn the emerald (B). There is in the song also the combination of the pseudorustic, the gathering of the pinions, with a stock allusion to the emotion of love, Love's arrows. But the shift from the rustic to the traditionally erotic is accomplished through juxtaposition of two basic human experiences: work and love. We could say that the two are also linked in terms of the "A, B" formula: while they are working (A), they would rather be loving (B). The link between the two choices is the use of the metaphors "pearls" (A) and "arrows" (B), each associated with a corresponding choice. That the one is hyperbolic—i.e., descriptive of the teeth used to break open the pinions—and that the other is standard—that the emotion of love is occasioned by Cupid's arrows is more a cliché than a productive metaphor—only serves to underline further the artificial nature of the rustic girl's song.

Even more surprising is the closing metaphor, which essentially repeats the expression of the choice between love and work. In lines 57–62, the song says that blind Cupid will be asking the sun for light for his eyes, while the girls are busy trampling the eyes of the sun (i.e., the patches of sunlight that filter through the pine trees) in the execution of their labors. The choice is here expressed chiasmatically in terms of the original formula, since love (B) is given before work (A) in these concluding lines. On one level, such a chiasmus would be simply another manifestation of artifice and an implicit rejection of parallelism (i.e., A,B; A,B), which is both more "natural" and, in Spain, reminiscent of an early and overworked poetic mode.[29] But the chiasmus, we venture to insist, is meant to bespeak a further hyperbole contained within the song, one in which the labors of the girls are seen to be on a higher plane than the activities of love, the latter such a worn concern of Western poetry by the late Renaissance. Although the girls themselves would typically prefer to exchange their work for love (lines 49–54), the song suggests that such a preference is ill-placed. The characterization of love in lines 57–62 is at the expense of the latter, as blind Cupid begs for sunlight in order to see that those very shepherdesses, their hair bright enough to provide light for the sun (line 20), scorn that sunlight by trampling it without concern in their routine if not idealized labors with the pinions. Therefore, the presence of Cupid and the presence of the suggested choice between him and rustic activities is far from a standard allusion in Góngora's poem. It is more significantly a hyperbolic device to imply the superiority of the girls over Cupid and the superiority, despite any standard sentiments which they might possess, of their pastoral labors over the labors of Love. Within this context, we may now understand the first "A, B" formula used in the poem, in lines 5–12. By saying that the shepherdesses that he sees in Xúcar are neither nymphs nor legions of Diana (*not* A), but are rather the best girls that Cuenca has to offer, the honor of that mountain, etc. (But rather B), is again not simply the poet's recourse to a standard hyperbole where his "reality" is superior to that of the tired symbols of classical mythology. It is an opening statement that suggests the intrinsic superiority of the girls' pastoral gay and abandoned activities to the emotions of love. While the latter are not explicitly denounced in the poem, in the fashion of the poet's general disenchantment with that human emotion (cf. our comments on the impact along these lines of the concluding verses of *Angélica and Medoro* or "Servía en Orán al Rey"), there is no question that both the narrator and the maidens—and this too becomes another unifying correlation in terms of the poem's interior duplication—see pastoral industry and diversion as superior to an insignificant, blind Cupid.

"En los pinares de Xúcar," as Dámaso Alonso has observed,[30] looks toward the *Solitudes* in its extremely decorative treatment of the pastoral setting. Our own presentation of the ballad would support such an affirmation, for we have seen how the poem exemplifies not only some major poetic concerns, manifested in the structural procedure of interior duplication, which lends a decidedly artificial and objective status to the composition, but also in the attitude toward the pastoral setting, in which one aspect of the decorative hyperboles becomes an implicit encomium of the superiority of the "simple" life over the deceits of blind Cupid. That the simple life is thus eulogized via a poetic structure that flaunts the inverisimilitude of its pseudonarrative framework is only a further portent of what Góngora is to do in the *Solitudes*.

CHAPTER 3

The Sonnets

DESPITE their wide popularity with anthologizers and compilers of introductions to Spanish literature, Góngora's 166 sonnets (plus fifty-two more attributed to him),[1] occupy somewhat of a limbo in terms of critical evaluations of his complete works. While the ballads studied in the preceding chapter and other short compositions (e.g., the *letrillas*) have received some attention for either their satirico-burlesque nature or for a combination of popular form with aristocratic Baroque thematics and language, and while the poet's enormous reputation seems based today primarily on the highly innovative compositions examined in our two chapters to follow, the sonnets, by virtue of their being by the late Renaissance one of the most traditional forms of lyrical expression, have been relatively neglected. Indeed, Robert Jammes, in his recent 701-page study of the poet and his works, devotes a scant twenty pages to these compositions of Petrarchan inspiration. His conclusion, that many of these compositions give an impression of *déja vu,*[2] while perhaps extreme, is nevertheless indicative of a general failure on the part of the critics to examine the sonnets in any fashion other than cursorily within general contexts.[3]

Nevertheless, the fact remains that a number of the sonnets are considered not only typical examples of Baroque poetry, but have as well, by virtue of their exposure in anthologies, come to be considered compositions of high literary merit. We cannot enter here into a discussion of one of the oldest chestnuts of literary history, the weight to be given originality of composition versus the meritorious handling of a traditional form. The sonnet by the late sixteenth century when Góngora begins to write (his earliest is dated 1582), is decidedly a traditional form, whereas the poet's longer compositions of the early seventeenth century constitute almost a genre of their own in Spanish poetry; at least they cannot be said to cause in the reader, either in language, structure, or theme, a sense of *déja vu* such as Jammes would attribute to the sonnets. Nevertheless, as the French critic observed in an earlier discussion of some of

Góngora's religious poetry (which he rightly finds execrable), the question is one more properly of good vs. bad poetry, with originality of attempt not necessarily correlating with either end of the qualitative spectrum. The question is, then, whether Góngora's sonnets are good—or whether even one or two are—and not whether as a totality they represent a new innovative direction in Baroque poetic form. While synthetic assessments and *apologiae* will continue to follow Dámaso Alonso's lead in demonstrating the mature brilliance of the longer compositions, during the time of the writing of which Góngora continued to compose sonnets (the last is dated 1624), any survey of his poetry that would focus on the intrinsic accomplishments of specific, "canonical" texts, as we pretend to do in this study, must characterize adequately those sonnets which have received so much attention, despite whatever the sonnets as a whole may exhibit. If for no other reason, the critic's commentary must contribute to the reader's understanding, precisely, of those compositions with which he is likely to come in contact in his study of Baroque Spanish poetry. Thus, again as in the case of the ballads, we select only a few of the recognizedly outstanding sonnets in order to submit them to a close scrutiny in terms of literary structure in general and Baroque aesthetics in particular.

I *An Early "Imitated" Sonnet*

E. Brockhaus,[4] in his generally ignored and somewhat unavailable study, divides his brief, running commentaries[5] on the sonnets into thirteen thematic and circumstantial groups: (1) sonnets on ladies and female beauty; (2) sonnets on poets and men of letters; (3) historical sonnets; (4) sonnets of praise; (5) sonnets of exhortation; (6) dirges; (7) sonnets on cities and churches; (8) votive sonnets; (9) religious sonnets; (10) philosophical sonnets; (11) miscellaneous sonnets; (12) sonnets contained in the dramas; (13) humorous and derisive sonnets. Brockhaus' first category refers basically to Góngora's first thirty-two sonnets, composed between 1582 and 1585 (Millé's nos. 216–47), a group characterized not only by an exclusive preoccupation with topics within the general realm of courtly love, but also by the persistent influence of and adherence to the Italian, Petrarchan tradition of love sonnets.[6] It is among this group, the compositions of which are quite uneven in quality, all raising questions concerning the critical evaluation of literary imitations, that the first two sonnets to be analyzed are found. Our first text has many points of contact with earlier Renaissance compositions[7]:

Mientras por competir con tu cabello,
oro bruñido al sol relumbra en vano,
mientras con menosprecio en medio el llano
mira tu blanca frente al lilio bello;
5 *mientras a cada labio, por cogello,*
siguen más ojos que al clavel temprano,
y mientras triunfa con desdén lozano
del luciente cristal tu gentil cuello;
goza cuello, cabello, labio y frente,
10 *antes que lo que fué en tu edad dorada*
oro, lilio, clavel, cristal luciente,
no sólo en plata o víola troncada
se vuelva, mas tú y ello juntamente
en tierra, en humo, en polvo, en sombra, en nada.[8]

(While gold burnished in the sun gleams in vain for competing with your hair; while your white brow regards with scorn the pretty lily fair in the middle of the plain; while more eyes pursue each lip, to pluck it, than follow the early carnation; and while your neck triumphs with haughty disdain for bright crystal; enjoy neck, hair, lip and brow, before what was in your golden youth gold, lily, carnation, shining crystal, not only turns into silver or plucked violet, but you and all this together turn into earth, into smoke, into dust, into shadow, into nothing.)[9]

Despite Brockhaus' isolation of a group of putatively "philosophical" sonnets, it should come as no surprise to the literate reader that Góngora's sonnet, like the majority of at least briefer lyrical compositions, reveals little in the way of noteworthy thematics. Indeed, the major preoccupation of a Baroque poet like Góngora, who even in his earliest compositions makes manifest the dominant concern with the matters of language and style that will characterize his most spectacular contributions to seventeenth-century poetry, is consistently in the realm of giving new and audacious form to what, in the isolation of critical summary, can seem none other than hackneyed clichés. Thus, Carballo Picazo has shown just how much of the raw material of the poem can be called commonplace in terms of the waning Western tradition of courtly love and feminine (imperative mood) and its unexpressed subject (*tú,* 'you') particularly these early ones, does reveal a rather depressing monotony. But poetry is more than thematics, as the literary critic cannot overemphasize, although the relatively facile search for meaning in literature—the reflection of an implied demand that literature in fact communicate, if not *be*, meaning—is probably too much a part of our intellectual heritage ever to be theorized away. Nevertheless, the attempt to reduce such works as this sonnet to meaning, including sources and internal allusions, cannot help but be prejudicial to a manifestation of Baroque literature which is first and foremost a form—to a relatively greater and lesser degree "pure" creative expression.

It is for this reason that one is able to dismiss so readily the "theme" of this sonnet. On the most basic level of literary commonplaces, the poet brings together the dual tradition of hyperbolic feminine idealization—the extravagant details of the woman's body, in particular the repeated affirmations that not only is the latter a perfection of nature, but rather it exceeds nature to such a degree that envy is produced—along with the imperative that such beauty must take advantage of the pleasures of life while it may. The latter is, of course, the commonplace of "gather ye rosebuds while ye may," better known in the European tradition as the Latin *collige rosas* from Ausonius' epigram. Both traditions may be given independent expression, and most assuredly repeatedly were, down the centuries. One may note, as a tentative approximation to Góngora's combining of the two (a combination in itself hardly unique since the sonnet may easily be compared to earlier texts in Spanish and Italian), that the sonnet as a whole is one extended period covering all fourteen verses. Thus, the natural break between the quatrains and the tercets corresponds to a syntactic break in the period between a compound conditional clause, broken into four parallel clauses introduced by *mientras* (since, while, because, etc.; lines 1, 3, 5, and 7), and the main clause of the sentence beginning with the first word of the first tercet (line 9), which is the main verb (imperative mood) and its unexpressed subject (*tú,* you) followed by another temporal/conditional clause which extends through the remaining five lines of the sonnet. In this fashion, the quatrains of the poem elaborate the commonplaces of idealized feminine beauty, while—and as an "emotional" result—the tercets express the *carpe diem* imperative, supported by the usual justification of such an imperative in the form of a reminder that such beauty is transitory and cannot endure. One original feature of Góngora's poem, as we shall demonstrate more extensively below, is not the casual combination of the two commonplaces, which are really placed side-by-side (quatrains vs. tercets), but the verbal overlapping of the two that provides an insistent structural unity. Graphically, we might represent as follows this complex poetic period: since A (Beauty), [lines 1–8)/then B (enjoy beauty), [line 9]/before *neg.* A (no beauty) [lines 10–14).

The whole point of representing the period that is the basic expressive unit of the sonnet so schematically is to highlight the symmetry involved. In reality, as can be seen, the imperative to the woman to enjoy her body is contained in only line 9 of the fourteen lines. Yet to the extent that the initial verse of the tercets is potentially one of the three most emphatic positions within a sonnet (along with the first and last lines), the impact of the main verb is hardly diminished. Indeed, the explicit tie-in of the imperative with the hyperbolic idealization of beauty in the quatrains through the "justification" of the last five lines may be made to give added weight to the urgency of that imperative. Clearly, the syntactic organization of Góngora's sonnet, which stresses a symmetry for the double "theme," is readily compared with an asymmetrical, perhaps more colloquial, disposition of the elements; since A and because *neg.* A, then B. We will have more to say concerning our poet's separation of the two dependent conditional clauses, for more than mere syntactic symmetry is involved. It is important, however, to note at this point that the second clause may be accurately described as conditional, despite its introduction of the "temporal" *antes que* (before). This is not the place to argue the semantic proximity of certain classes of temporal and conditional clauses. Suffice it to say that the injunction "do B before A happens" carries with it the strong implication, if not the certainty, of "do B, because A will happen subsequently."

The two quatrains of the sonnet deserve some concentrated attention for the form in which the idealized beauty of the unknown woman is expressed. Dámaso Alonso has written several times on the expressive pattern of these verses, a pattern which he has shown to be an integral part not only of Góngora's poetic style, but of the entire Petrarchan tradition as well. The reader's attention is first called to the presence of a reiterative pattern by the repetition of the conjunction *mientras* (since) four times in eight lines; more specifically, to introduce the four oddly-numbered lines of the quatrains. Closer examination reveals that the result of such a repetition is a polymembration of the opening conditional clause into four compound subclauses which function together on an equal semantic footing to make up an abstract whole, which is the hyperbolic suggestion of the woman's beauty. Each member of this compound clause emphasizes one synecdochal aspect of that beauty; her hair (line one), her forehead (line four), her lips (line five, her neck (line eight).

Two passing comments are necessary here. First, Góngora follows a commonplace classical tradition of describing the woman from the "top" down; but in this case, although he moves from feature to feature in order, in the end he has only really described her head and its neck. Thus, while the four features are themselves synecdochal (and notice the absence of reference to the eyes, in other contexts the paradigmatic human feature, the "windows of the soul"), the final whole is in turn only suggestively synecdochal of the entire human form of the woman. We should also point out the symmetry of the mention of the four features. Each feature belongs to one of the subclauses introduced by the reiterative *mientras.* Furthermore, each feature is contrasted conceitfully with a manifestation of nature which is supposedly prototypic of perfect brilliance and/or beauty. Thus, the hair outshines polished gold vainly gleaming in the sun; the forehead can look with disdain upon the lilies of the field; each lip attracts more eyes than the early carnation; the neck triumphs with haughty disdain over shining crystal. Aside from the system of comparisons themselves, the structure of each subclause is noteworthy. For example, in the case of members one and three, the human feature occurs in the first verse of the two-verse subclause; while in the case of members two and four, the human feature is not mentioned until the second of the two verses. On the other hand, in the case of features one and three, the latter are the "objects," so to speak, of vain competition by the point of comparison: in order to compete with your hair, polished gold shines in vain; in order to pick them, more eyes follow each one of your lips than the early carnation. But in the case of features two and four, the actual feature is the subject of an active verb, of which the point of comparison is the object: both forehead and neck disdain, in turn, lilies and crystal.

This is more than just poetic acrobatics. If each one of the four members were structured in an identical fashion, the result would be what in Spanish is known as "parallelistic" poetry, is associated with the early Medieval and "primitive" lyric.[10] The most significant use of parallelistic poetry, so that the reader may have a point of reference, would appear to be religious litanies, where whole series of phrases enjoy identical syntactical arrangement. The effect of such a procedure, obviously, is quite removed from the complex, pseudo-Latinate syntax which Góngora and other Baroque poets were interested in imposing upon the Spanish language. The result of such structuring may be quite far removed from the colloquial standard of either seventeenth- or twentieth-century Spanish. And this is precisely the point: the quatrains may be expressing hyperbolically some rather standard commonplaces concerning human beauty; the reader is meant not to evaluate the commonplaces but rather the systematic patterning by which they are expressed. One important aspect of such a procedure is that the inexperienced reader is unable at first and superficial reading to grasp the syntax and the semantics of the compound clauses. Both the patterning and its lack of simple parallelistic expression force upon him a concentrated deciphering of structure. This is the "objective" goal of Baroque poetry which we mentioned previously—the attempt to focus the reader's attention on the poem as an autonomous and complex artistic object.

As far as concerns the pairs of correlations established in the quatrains, the following tercets, which, as we have already demonstrated, focus on the hedonistic imperative to the woman to enjoy her youth, return to the features as well as the comparisons. The return to these double members in the temporal/conditional clause appended as justification to the imperative serves both to tie the two clauses together "across" the imperative of line 9, so to speak, and, more importantly, to provide an overall structural unity for the composition. Thus, in line 9, which is introduced by the key command *goza* (enjoy), there are four objects to the verb; i.e., the four human features. Here, the four are simply enumerated. But note that the enumeration is not in the original order of presentation in lines 1–8; that is, their repetition does not follow a parallelistic pattern of reference, and, in terms of the original order, their order in line 9 is 4, 1, 3, 2. It would be difficult to justify this latter order. Certainly, it suggests somewhat of a mirror image, and a simple mathematical formula could probably be written to derive 4, 1, 3, 2 from 1, 2, 3, 4; but then this might be true of any random rearrangement of the original members, and the only meaningful justification might be that *frente* must occur last in line 9 in order to rhyme with lines 11 and 13. But then, rhyme is never much of a profound justification for poetic structure, particularly where serious literature is involved. What we are left with, therefore, is simply another example of the avoidance of facile parallelisms. In terms of the initial correlation between human features and points of reference in nature, the occurrence in line 9 as objects of the imperative verb of the human features reintroduces the basic correlation, which is carried out by the reintroduction of the points of reference in nature in line 11. Again, the repetition of members from the quatrains is not predictable; where the woman's features are scrambled in line 9, the invidious nonhuman elements are presented in their original order. Therefore, if we can speak of two sets of related correlations, one in the quatrains and one in the first tercet, and if we represent the human features by X and the nonhuman elements by Y, with subsigns for the four-part distribution, we have the following pattern (the prime represents the second occurence of the correlation):

quatrains: X_1 (hair)/Y_1 (gold)
X_2 (forehead)/Y_2 (lilies)
X_3 (lips)/Y_3 (carnation)
X_4 (neck)/Y_4 (crystal)

first tercet: $'X_4/'X_1/'X_3/'X_2$
$'Y_1/'Y_2/'Y_3/'Y_4$

On the basis of the correlation alone between the woman's envious features and invidious elements of nature, there is a tight structural unity between quatrains and tercets, between the two traditional commonplaces represented in the sonnet and between the two conditional clauses which together function to provoke the emphatic imperative and to justify its urgency.

However, we have yet to characterize both the most stunning and the most complex aspect of the sonnet. In the first place, after the reiteration of the major correlation of the composition, line 12 presents a bimembrational object of the main verb of the second clause: enjoy X_{1-4} before . . . Y_{1-4} become "silver or plucked violet . . ." There is a complex conceit underlying this much of the second clause appended to the imperative. On the one hand, both the woman's beauty and the nonhuman elements used to highlight it hyperbolically are spoken of as being in their "golden age," presumably a reference to the Classical concept of the Golden Age, the summit of ideal perfection. The imperative is meant to obtain before that golden age wanes, before both the complex X as well as the complex Y become "silver or plucked violet." That they will become silver seems to play on the idea of a golden age—the silver age is a debasement of the perfection of the former. And at the same time, at least one of the woman's points of beauty, her hair, is associated with shining gold: the brighter-than-gold hair of her youth will become the duller silver hair of age. But on the other hand, at least two of the other features, her forehead and her lips, outdo nature's flowers, are in a certain sense more flowers than nature's own. This in youth; but in age—and in death—they will become "plucked violets," not only the flower of death, but also, in being plucked, separated from the source of life (note that the Spanish uses a verb closer to "truncated, torn out" than the less emphatic "plucked"). In this sense, "silver" and "plucked violet" refer conceitfully not only to the several features and elements, but also to both halves of the original correlation, and we can extend our graphic representation of the pattern of correlations as follows (the double prime represents the reiteration of the correlation):

second tercet: 1. 12: $''XY_{1-4}$

By running X and Y together and by not specifying a distribution for the subsigns representing the four elements, we indicate the fusion of all eight in the two members that constitute the first objects of the "become" in line 13.

But the last two lines of the sonnet go on to provide an alternate set of objects for the verb "become," and thus a further extension of the basic correlation. And if in the case of "silver or plucked violet" the four pairs are confused in two symbols, in line 14 the four are spread out among five separated elements. As Dámaso Alonso has noted,[11] it would be futile to attempt to correlate the five with any one of the basic four pairs of elements introduced in the quatrains. Some sort of superficial approximation is possible, but no decisive assignment can be made: "shadow" might refer to "crystal" but then again it might refer to "hair," since the latter is referred to along with gold shining in the sun, and so on. In reality, all five are meant to refer synthetically to the original four pairs:

second tercet: 1.14: $'''XY_{1-4}$

Actually, there are two ways to understand the dramatic *accumulatio* that Góngora provides in this stunning conclusion to his hedonistic imperative. Our original reading of the sonnet was based on the attempt to see a perpetuation of the four-part division of the elements of the composition. In this sense, although the first four elements of line 14 ("earth, smoke/humus, dust, shadow") cannot be assigned securely to the several X and Y pairs, there is the suggestion of a corresponding, fateful transformation provided for each one of the original ideal elements. And together, the four culminate synthetically in the brutal impact of the last word, "nothing" (which could then be indicated as a fifth statement of the correlation collapsed in one word: $''''XY_{1-4}$). Our impression is now, however, that the five words that make up the last line are meant to represent one synthetic reiteration of the correlation and that there is a *gradatio*, a progressive movement, from one word to the next. If we see *humo* as meaning more humus in a pseudo-biblical sense of the earth from which human flesh is made and to which it will return in death,[12] rather than assigning the word its more current meaning of "smoke," we can appreciate the movement from the more concrete to the more disperse and abstract. Both beauty (X) and nature (Y) will, despite whatever superiority of the former over the latter, in the end together become by swift degrees the nothing that is the only permanent reality of cosmic existence. *Nada* is, in this reading, not the synthesis of the preceding four elements, but the final transformation of matter, as in the end it must revert to its primeval nonbeing.

Aside from the customary observation that this conclusion to the rather standard deployment of the themes of ideal beauty and *carpe diem* reflects the putative general cynicism of the Baroque period as well as whatever can be called Góngora's own personal bleak and thoroughly non-Christian pessimism concerning the permanence of ideals (in the neoplatonic Christian tradition, beauty at least continues to exist in the mind of God and nothingness therefore has no metaphysical-theological validity), it is important to note what has happened to the structure of the patterned correlation. Whereas at the outset of the sonnet we are able to discern a clear division between two poles of a correlation (X and Y) and a precise characterization of four paired elements, in the second clause which closes the sonnet, we have seen that in at least two reiterations, the eight elements of the correlation are merged into symbols which bespeak the strident note on which the sonnet will end. This is significant to the degree that Góngora is consciously striving to show that, although on a hypothetic and hyperbolic level, one can leisurely make the paired comparisons with which the sonnet opens, when faced with the reason that ideal beauty must hedonistically partake of life, when faced with the inescapable reality of human decay and death, such careful distinctions no longer obtain, and all fuse together in the face of the *nada* which is the only enduring characteristic of life and human experience. While one can call this confusion of elements typically Baroque—the refutation of the neat compartments to which the universe is reduced by an earlier Aristotelian and scholastic philosophy—it is more important to see the function of the various occurrences of the initial correlation throughout in terms of an attempt to give a dense structural unity to a poetic text. Unity is provided by the persistent reiteration of the correlation for both of the themes presented and, more significantly, by the final fusion of all of the elements of the correlation in terms of one highly symbolic string of phrases whose final member, *nada*, "nothing," comes to overshadow the entire composition.

II *Structure in a Topical Sonnet*

The foregoing analysis of one sonnet, despite its unusual length in a general introduction to Góngora such as this proposes to be, was necessary in order to demonstrate how the sonnets, even the early ones, can be approached more productively from the point of view of literary structure rather than superficial thematics. Our next sonnet is also a well-known composition from among the early works on topics of courtly love:

> *La dulce boca que a gustar convida*
> *un humor entre perlas destilado*
> *y a no invidiar aquel licor sagrado*
> *que a Júpiter ministra el garzón de Ida,*
> 5 *amantes no toquéis si queréis vida;*
> *porque entre un labio y otro colorado*
> *Amor está de su veneno armado,*
> *cual entre flor y flor sierpe escondida.*
> *No os engañen las rosas, que a la Aurora*
> 10 *diréis que aljofaradas y olorosas,*
> *se le cayeron del purpúreo seno.*
> *Manzanas son de Tántalo, y no rosas,*
> *que después huyen del que incitan ahora,*
> *y sólo del Amor queda el veneno.*[13]

(The sweet mouth that invites tasting of a liquid distilled among pearls, and invites no envy for that sacred liquor which the youth from Ida administers to Jupiter—lovers, don't touch it if you want life; because between one and another red lip lies Love, armed with his poison, like a serpent hidden between one and another flower. Don't be deceived by the roses, which at Dawn you could say fell, pearled and fragrant, from the purple bosom. They are Tantalus' apples, and not roses, which later flee from him whom they now incite, and only the poison of Love is left behind.[14])

Without stressing a diametrical opposition, we may say preliminarily that in this sonnet Góngora contradicts to a great extent the hedonistic imperative so insistently expressed in the preceding poem. Like the latter, this poem is also built on a series of imperatives; but, rather than positive, they are now negative (lines 5, 9; this is more properly an indirect command, but no less an imperative functionally: "may you not be deceived . . ." = "don't be deceived . . . "). Although paraphrase is rarely an acceptable approach to a poetic text, the Baroque complexity of Góngora's poem suggests such a summary as an initial approximation to the expression of that negative imperative: Lovers are told *not* to touch, if they want "life" (possibly in the Christian spiritual sense of grace; more likely in the metaphorical sense of peace and tranquility per commonplaces of courtly love), the sweet mouth that invites them to its sensual liquid on the one hand (perhaps a metonymy for the entire sexual experience; perhaps a synecdoche of all physical pleasure, if not a quite explicit allusion to the locus of that experience) and which, on the other hand, invites them *not* to envy the sacred nectar proffered to Jupiter by Ganymedes (supposedly because the liquid of the sweet mouth is understandably more inviting than the sacred nectar associated with the homosexual, platonic relationship between Jupiter and his cupbearer). Do not, the narrative voice continues, touch that mouth, for between the two lips, as the serpent hides among the flowers (a commonplace from Vergil's *Second Eclogue*), Love armed with poison (a conceit built on the reference to Cupid being armed with the arrows which provoke the sensation of love that in the end works like poison upon the lover) is hiding. Lovers, do not be deceived by the roses (that is, by the woman's red lips) which you would probably say had fallen "pearled" (by dew) and fragrant from Dawn's purple breast. *Rather,* they are the apples of Tantalus, and not roses, and (thus) they end up fleeing from the one that they have incited, and the lover, having tasted the roses (having been pierced by Love's poisoned arrows), is left after their flight with only their poison. (The latter is an allusion, beyond the poison of Love's arrows, to the commonplace, used in religious literature by virtue of the apple's long association with the forbidden fruit of the Garden of Eden, that the apple may be rotten, poisoned, but still remains fragrant and attractive.)

Although the reader has available the prose translation of the sonnet, the foregoing paraphrase points to some of the references of Góngora's conceitful language, as well as to some of the subtle relationships that are meant to be discerned between elements that, at first glance, are somewhat disparate. The sonnet is most assuredly a case in point of how literature has no relationship to logical, expository writing. For example, the reader is presented with at least three different sets of unrelated allusions: Jupiter and Ganymedes (associated with nonphysical, homosexual love); Love and his poisoned arrows, lying in wait like the prototypic snake in the grass; Tantalus and his frustrated appetites which may be to the point here, but which traditionally are associated with a punishment by the gods for nonamorous reasons. A dominant characteristic of the poem is not only the presence of these sets, but also the abrupt movement from one to another with little explanatory transition, with the reader left to contemplate the juxtaposition and to extract as he will the significance of that juxtaposition. Thus, as we shall see in a moment, some problem of interpretation is involved in the reference to Jupiter and Ganymedes in the first quatrain.

It has been customary for criticism to stress Góngora's inspiration for this poem in Torquato Tasso's sonnet "Quel labbro che le rose han colorito" ("That lip which the roses have colored").[15] Nathan Gross has commented as follows on this tendency to dismiss a poem too lightly because of its superficial resemblance to—and/or direct inspiration in—another composition:

> If this tradition [of dismissing the sonnet because it is an "imitation"] of over three hundred years' standing is grounded in truth, then Góngora, in 1584, was simply turning an Italian poem into his own Castilian idiom. Whatever beauty or lesson may be extracted from the sonnet was not original with him; and aside from the reader's interest in watching the early Góngora translate and in guessing at which elements of the later Góngora are already beginning to develop, there is no reason for attempting to grasp the intuitions expressed in the poem: since they are Tasso's, not Góngora's, it is more satisfactory to discern them in their original, and equally beautiful form . . .
>
> Both works are indeed tinged with *amargo desengaño* [bitter disillusionment]; and the fruit of Tantalus, the hidden serpent, the rose-colored lip are images Góngora has imitated from Tasso. But disillusion is the common property of the Spanish Baroque; Góngora did not need Tasso to supply this theme. And the poetic figures he borrowed, which form Tasso's whole stock in his sonnet, are not merely copies: they are integrated into an entirely new system of imagery of a far more complex and subtle set of statements on the disillusions of life.[16]

Gross goes on to give a religio-moral interpretation of the sonnet that is unique to Góngora's handling of the "borrowed" material. Although he does not say so explicitly, Gross's essay is informed by the belief of more recent schools of literary criticism which stress the unity of a literary work: although every element of a work may be borrowed from some other work—themes, language, metaphors—a unique elaboration of the borrowing confers upon that work an independent, autonomous standing as an artistic object.

As we have attempted to underline in our clumsy paraphrase, Góngora's sonnet presents a negative imperative to lovers via a rather complex mingling of apparently disparate elements. Any interest of the sonnet to the mature reader must be, not the theme itself—any anthology of Baroque poetry would reveal dozens of examples of similarly cynical denunciations of love's attractions—but its elaboration in terms of an "inner logic" that binds the disparate elements into a convincing whole. Said in another way, in order to assign an artistic importance to Góngora's sonnet, the critic must discover the network of relationships that support and give conviction to the central negative imperative which is the focal point of the poem. In order to do this, we will resort to the following graphic representation of the network of relationships involved. Many readers of criticism are antagonistic to such a device, perhaps feeling that the discussion of humanistic phenomena is only able to maintain the artistic aura of a work through its presentation in discursive prose. Yet, and with all due deference to the feeling that schemata may interpose a dehumanizing emotional barrier between the reader and the work they pretend to describe, the characteristic complexity of relationships involved in many a Baroque poem can efficiently and effectively be shown only via such a device. In the following representation, the Roman numerals refer to the four stanzas, while the Arabic numerals simply identify major verbal elements. Those elements which are explicit to the sonnet are simply listed; those which are implied are enclosed in square brackets. The slash represents the line of progression for each trimembrational set (in the case of the first stanza, the sets are 1/2/3 and 1/4/5; that is, the mouth's inviting has a double complement, "to enjoy" and "not to envy . . ."); each set can be seen to be reducible more or less to a simple sentence, and the three members of each set consist of the subject, verb, and object of such a putative simple sentence:

I.	1. mouth		
	/		
	2. enjoy	——	4. not envy
	/		/
	3. Love's humor		5. Jupiter's sacred nectar
II.	6. mouth	[=]	9. flowers
	/		/
	7. hides		10. hide
	/		/
	8. Love's poison		11. serpent [of sin?]

III. 12. roses [i.e., mouth]
/
13. appear
/
14. from Dawn's breast

[=]IV. 15. Tantalus' apples
/
16. flee
/
17. from incited object

[=]18. Love
/
19. only leaves
/
20. poison

Stephen Booth has shown in a recent study of Shakespeare how complex sonnets such as the ones written by the Englishman reveal a number of different superimposed patterns, rather than the one merely linear pattern of the normal reading experience.[17] Any adequate understanding of the artistic complexity of Shakespeare's sonnets must, therefore, be based on an identification of these superimposed patterns as well as an understanding of how they function in relationship to each other. Booth has at his disposal more space than we do, but the implications of his approach to the present discussion of one of Góngora's sonnets are obvious. Given the foregoing paraphrase and graphic representation, and assuming that both are accurate, we may refer to at least four major groups of relationships—patterns, if you will—that occur within the sonnet. The elements of each group are identified by the number used in the graph in order to save space:

1. Direct Relationships: $1=6=12$; $3=5$ [in part]; $6=9$; $12=15=18$; $3=8=20=11$
2. Antithetical Relationships: $3\neq 8, 20$; $5\neq 11$; $5\neq 15$(?); $14\neq 17, 20$; $2\neq 7, 19$; $2\neq 4$; $3\neq 5$ [in part]
3. Metaphorical Movement: $1, 6=12$; $6=9, 8=11$; $12=15=18$
4. Rhymed Coupling: *humor . . . destilado/licor sagrado; Ida/vida; vida/serpiente escondida; purpúreo seno/veneno; convida/vida; colorado/armado*

These four sets of relationships are all fairly tangible, and we exclude more subtle and less obvious patterns such as stress and other phonetic phenomena, syntactical and grammatical symmetry, etc., since the full appreciation of these phenomena depends on a thorough grasp of the Spanish language. The first group, Direct Relationships, concerns both semantic pairing, such as the two occurrences of "mouth," as well as metaphoric pairing (implied semantic equivalence), such as the identification of "mouth" and "flowers." This first set essentially involves those elements which are directly equated as part of the "givens" concerning the nature of human love. The second set, Antithetical Relationships, is essentially an extension of the first, but is concerned with coupling of inversely related elements, either those which are brought together because they are sensed to be fundamentally equal ("Love's humor" and "Love's poison"), or elements which are juxtaposed in order to highlight the disillusionment which is the main thrust of the poem ("red roses" and "Tantalus' apples"). The third set focuses more explicitly on the major metaphoric elements, although one could easily argue that the entire poem is a metaphor and therefore the noting of individual metaphors is redundant. The "mouth" and "roses" juxtaposition is an implied metaphor; had we more space we would dwell in detail on the importance of the occurrence of the two phrases in identical positions ("mouth" in the opening line of the quatrains; "roses" in the opening lines of the tercets) in calling our attention to a possible metaphoric relationship. Suffice it to say that such "syntactic coupling" is a frequent manifestation of implied metaphors.[18]

The fourth group is concerned with another form of coupling, Rhymed Coupling, where the participation of elements in the same rhyme scheme is also a frequent device to call attention to their relationship, either "direct" or antithetical. Thus, it is no accident that the phrases for "Love's humor" and "Jupiter's sacred nectar" rhyme: the relationship between them is in part direct (both are related to a form of amorous attachment between two persons), and in part antithetical (on the one hand, because human love has nothing to envy in homosexual, Platonic love; on the other hand, because the love evoked by the sweet mouth is human, while the love associated with the nectar is of the gods). Or, to take another example, "life" and the metonymic reference to Ganymedes (*vida* and *Ida*) rhyme, thus reinforcing the dichotomy between human love (and its dangerous, disruptive threat to "life") and the tranquil and eternal love of the gods.

Thus, the poem presents little difficulty of interpretation. We have insisted, instead, that the major interest of the composition is more properly any unique, inner "poetic logic" that provides the complex, objective autonomy associated with Baroque literature. Nathan Gross, in his detailed examination of the poem, has raised an interpretational difficulty, however. Gross would see in the reference to Jupiter, "life," Tantalus' apples, the serpent, etc., a network of religious or quasi-religious symbology, whereby Góngora is imploring the lovers to flee physical love because it is sinful, an offense to the gods, who will punish the lovers with the eternal torment of Tantalus. Perhaps if Gross were to have pursued his interpretation on a purely metaphorical level and not have had recourse to Edenic symbology and to Christian values,[19] we could agree with him. But as Robert Jammes has convincingly demonstrated, Góngora's interest in religious values is embarrassing to anyone who would see the Counter-Reformation as the whole basis of the Spanish Baroque (as would Helmut Hatzfeld), and it is not surprising to find assessments of Góngora's work which attempt to demonstrate that the attacks against him and his literature were based less on the complex nature of his verbal art than on the unabashed amorality of his poetic world.[20] There is, in short, a world of difference between Lope de Vega's contemporary *Rimas sacras* (*Sacred Poems* [i.e., sonnets]) and Góngora's poetry. That the sonnet under consideration is a "denunciation" of human, physical love is undeniable; that such love is to be denounced because it is a "sin" against God or the gods is more questionable. We have already suggested, in our paraphrase, that the function of the reference to Jupiter is to emphasize the attraction of "Love's humor" (i.e., saliva) by both comparing it to "Jupiter's sacred nectar" and by implying that for the lovers the latter has no attraction when compared to the former: heterosexual human love is more attractive, despite its dangers and deception, than homosexual Platonic love. The rhymed coupling of "life" and "Ida's youth" is simply a reinforcement of this complex comparison-contrast, and we nowhere see in the sonnet the poet's desire to suggest that, in following the advice to flee the traps of human love, the lovers should substitute the latter with Jupiter's amatory preferences, or even that human love is offensive to the latter. While Gross's interpretation of the sonnet recommends itself for the attempt to demonstrate the autonomy of Góngora's poem from the Tasso original, it is probably inaccurate in wanting to unify all of the references of the sonnet into one synthetic conceit. We have argued, on the other hand, that the sonnet, as is the case with much of Góngora's poetry (see the following two chapters), deploys disparate allusions and elements for their emphatic value within shifting patterns of relationships without any necessary final resolution into one overriding symbolic meaning. This is the case with this sonnet as it was with the first sonnet examined in this chapter, where the numerous references given throughout the composition possess less an intrinsic progressive meaning than they do a circumstantial extrinsic meaning imposed by the correlational pattern.

III *The Use of Conceit in the Sonnet*

Although within the broader perspective of Góngora's complete poetry, one may want to argue that the Cordoban's love sonnets do not rank among his most original and innovative works, consideration of two indicative selections, we have insisted, is imposed by the wide diffusion of the texts as well as by their intrinsic complexity. The presence of that complexity alone demonstrates the degree to which Góngora infused these supposedly more marginal compositions with his own individual Baroque aesthetic. Our next two compositions may also be grouped together on the basic general thematic orientation. Both deal with death: the first is the third of three sonnets on the occasion of the catafalque erected in Córdoba to the memory of the Queen, Margarita of Austria, who died in 1611; the second is an "inscription for the sepulcher of Dominico Greco," the painter, and is dated 1614. Both demonstrate not only the putative Baroque interest in topics of death, but also reveal once again Góngora's bringing together within the unifying context of the brief sonnet a series of highly disparate and only barely fusible image-conceits.

The first sonnet, on the catafalque to Margarita, is variously dated 1611 or 1612, the former date being now the more preferred:

Máquina funeral, que desta vida
nos decís la mudanza estando queda,
pira, no de aromática arboleda,
si a más gloriosa Fénix construída.

5 *Bajel en cuya gavia esclarecida*
estrellas, hijas de otra mejor Leda,
serenan la Fortuna, de su rueda
la volubilidad reconocida,
farol luciente sois, que solicita
10 *la razón, entre escollos naufragante*
al puerto; y a pesar de lo luciente,
oscura concha de una Margarita,
que, rubí en caridad, en fe diamante
renance en nuevo Sol en nuevo oriente.[21]

(Funeral machine, you who tell us of the mutability of this life while remaining still, pyre, not from the aromatic grove, but for a more glorious Phoenix constructed. You are a vessel in whose illustrious topsail stars—the daughters of another, better Leda—makes Fortune serene, the volubility of whose wheel is well known, [and you are] a beacon which beckons reason, going shipwrecked on the reefs, to shore; and despite the light, a dark conch of a Margarita [pearl], who, a ruby in charity and a diamond in faith, will be reborn in a new Sun in a new East.[22])

R. O. Jones, after discussing the superior relationship of this text to the two preceding sonnets on the same subject (both also dated 1611; the first lacks a desired unity, while the second is excessively complex even for Góngora), goes on to schematize the poem's images as follows:

The *túmulo,* an unmoving symbol of mutability, A
is the pyre (suggested by the candles) of a better Phoenix. B
It is like a ship assured of divine favour by
St. Elmo's fire; its lights make it,
through a paradox, into a lighthouse beckoning to harbour.
Hence it stands for both stillness and movement. A_1
It is a shell from which the Queen will be reborn into
a new life (like the Phoenix from its pyre).[23] B_1

Jones, however, does not discuss in detail either the basis for his identification of two pairs of major elements, nor does he demonstrate how the rapid succession of points of reference (allusions, images, metaphoric comparisons) fuse into the higher unity of a poetic structure. For example, one of the basic conceits of the poem concerns the reference to the Phoenix bird. Margarita herself, in a not unexpected flight of elegiac hyperbole, is called a more glorious Phoenix (line 4), and in the last line it is stated that the Queen will rise again from the shell (conch) of the catafalque, to be reborn under a new Sun, in a new East. The reference here is surely to the Christian symbology of the Phoenix, whose resurrection is customarily understood as both the Resurrection of Christ as well as the promise of a Second Coming. Although Góngora cannot be called a religious poet (see our rejection of Eve symbology in the discussion of the preceding sonnet), given the elegiac context for the Christian Queen of the country which saw itself the defender of the faith, the use of such references for conceitful poetic purposes, without any significant attempt to dwell on their validity, can be taken as normal poetic rhetoric. Thus the importance of the reference is not its religious value, but its role in unifying the hyperbolic identification of the dead Queen. In this case, the two references to the Phoenix, the identification of the "burning pyre" of the catafalque and its candles with the literal pyre from which the bird is reborn, serve as the principal focus of the elegy. Margarita is not merely a manifestation of the Phoenix myth (*not,* according to line 3, the real bird's aromatic grove). She is more glorious and will be reborn by virtue of the new promise of Christ, which transcends the old promise of the pre-Christian myth.

This comparison is an old ingredient of Christian poetic rhetoric, conscious as part of its cultural background of the relationship between pagan belief and the Old Testament on the one hand, and the renewed promises of the New Testament on the other.[24] As we stated, Góngora is less interested in religious symbology than he is in poetic conceits, and in this case he is able, via his references to the Phoenix, not only to rephrase the Christian promise of the rebirth of the soul at the time of the Last Judgment, but also to justify the conceit of line 2. That the dead woman's tomb is able "to tell us of change while being still" can be taken on one level to refer to the medieval commonplaces of the Death which brings the permanency of the grave to all through the inevitable changes of life from which none can escape. But on another level, the phrase can be seen to bespeak the "changes" to which man will be subject beyond the apparent permanency of his interment; to wit, final judgment and resurrection of the soul of the saintly. These references, which cover the opening and closing stanza, have then a Christological significance and allude to the undisputed saintliness of the departed consort. Indeed, one could, with little violation of the sense of the conceits, argue that an equiparence is in fact implied between Margarita and Christ himself,[25] an implication undoubtedly resting on the farther reaches of hyperbole, but one which is not altogether inappropriate to the emphatic contexts of a Baroque poetry which undertakes to impose its vision upon the reader through the effectiveness of its own inner logic. One should also note the chiasmatic phrasing in line 13 of the metaphoric allusion to the woman's virtues. The ruby and the diamond (and see again note 25) can probably be argued to possess Christological meaning (certainly the latter has a long history of reference to the "luminous being" and the ruby is with ease correlated with the blood of the Savior). Whether such is their function in the poem is impossible to state with certainty. The presence of the double epithet of Christian virtue plus her very name is, however, given emphasis by its penultimate position, its hyperbatonic interruption of the clause which begins with the first word of the verse and continues with the next and last verse, and by the structure of chiasmus by which the epithet is expressed: X/in Y, in Y/X.

The two inner stanzas of the sonnet (it should be apparent by now that the movement of the sonnet does not follow the traditional balancing of quatrains and tercets) continue what can be called conceitful Christian symbology, again not out of any spirit of piety, but simply as an effective form of poetic elegy. The second stanza takes up the ship metaphor of Christianity, reinforcing it by the presence of the candles, which are identified as guiding stars. The line of thought is confused and difficult here, but one's attention is immediately caught by the mention of "daughters of another, better Leda." The implication of this assertion is again a juxtaposition between pagan myth and Christian beliefs. The "daughters" of Leda are the stars (feminine in Spanish), Castor and Pollux, the augurs of safe arrival for ships. But the candles which light Margarita's catafalque are, we suggest, meant to be seen as her "daughters," which augur the safe arrival of this ship's passenger, the Queen—i.e., her final union with Christ, the only redeeming promise of terrestrial death (a point brought out more explicitly in the first sonnet of the series: *en polvo ya el clarín final espera* [in dust the final clarion she awaits]).[26] This interpretation is based on the reference to Leda, which may be understood in one of two ways, which are probably meant to be fused conceitfully.

The most immediate understanding of the "other, better Leda" is the Virgin Mary, the mother of Christ (who is often correlated, along with his "twin" brother, St. James the Minor—Spain's Santiago de Compostela—with Castor and Pollux in some popular Christian beliefs[27]). Thus, through the gift to mankind of the Virgin, her Son, mankind has a new more powerful star to guide him safely to his final port, ultimate union with God. Another, more audacious way of understanding the allusion is in terms of a prevalent custom of seeing the Virgin, and her "daughters," the exemplary virtuous women of Christianity, as equally important as Christ (cf. the sense of Gonzalo de Berceo's Marian literature). Thus the new Leda may well be meant to be understood as Margarita, who in death, as in life, is meant to be a guiding light to mankind. This is certainly a fitting and routine affirmation for an elegy. The point of all this is not so much the clarification of the exact meaning of the allusions in the sonnet, but the necessary dwelling, in inevitable detail, on the sort of shifting and ambiguous images with which Góngora's Baroque art is constructed. The overall effect, even for a trained reader, is often one of maddening frustration as to what, exactly, the poet is getting at. Often what he is getting at is simply an ingenious complexity based on a dazzling grasp of the potential of the poetic conceit, the sustained image that can have no support in external reality or logic. Once the reader can follow the gist of such a procedure, learning to adjust quickly to the central shifts in emphasis and reference, the reading of Góngora's poetry is somewhat more of an interesting experience. The use of religious—semireligious or pseudoreligious—symbology in this sonnet, like some of the more pedestrian allusions of the previous two love sonnets, is a good example of the rhetorical premises upon which at least the sonnets rest.

The second quatrain concludes with another reference to the matter of change, this time via the mention of Fortune and her famous wheel. This second reference, tied as it is to the religious meaning of the stars and Leda, both recalls the mention of change in line 2 as well as gives support to our assertion that the "change" referred to is double in meaning, with allusion to man's fickle terrestrial fate and, on a higher level, to the transformation of his soul beyond the tomb of earthly death. Concatenating the symbolic images of his elegy, the stars of the second quatrain become the beacon of the first tercet. Such a shift, like the second reference to change with the introduction of Fortune in line 7, may serve to clarify an earlier, related allusion. In this case, we may refer back to the mention of Leda. That the catafalque is now a beacon reinforces, at least at this point, the understanding of the "new Leda" as an antonomastic reference to the example which the dead Queen may constitute for her subjects and all mankind. The verb which appears as the third word of line 9, and which is incidentally the main verb of the single period of the entire sonnet, refers, not to Margarita herself, but to her catafalque. "Funeral machine" in the opening verse is the subject of this verb (thus note that in this way there is, in fact, a division on one level between the quatrains and the tercets: the former contain the subject of the period and its appositions, while the latter contain the predicate and its members). But there can be little doubt that the focus of the sonnet is less an inscription for the physical monument than it is an elegy for the remains contained within. Indeed, the catafalque and its physical presence have become symbolically a complex metonymy for Margarita: the monument, the candles, interment itself—all refer to the virtues of the woman and the promise of salvation which in death she bespeaks as an ideal saint of Christian faith. This third tercet makes quite explicit the guiding function of the woman and her death: the vessel of her remains bears lights which are to guide the shipwrecked sinner to port. In this way, Margarita in death assumes as much a role as a symbolic savior of mankind as does Christ in traditional Christian belief. Whether this is heretical is beside the point: one can find numerous such hyperbolic elegies in the literature of the period and before, particularly within a context that supported the belief in the choice by the Almightly of specific individuals—monarchs, churchmen, saints—to interpret His will on earth.

The double point of reference of the poem—to the physical catafalque and to the symbolic function of its contents—is brought out by the virtual oxymoron spread over part of lines 11 and 12: "despite that which is glowing (the candles, their point of reference, their promise, etc.), dark shell . . . (the unlit interior of the catafalque, the dark night of earthly death of the Queen, etc.)." The juxtaposition of these antithetical elements of light at this point—and light is a focal point for the transcendent function of the dead woman: the stars, the beacon of the sinner—serves to recall, as we move into the final summary of the saintliness of the Margarita who will renew the promise of Christ in her own final resurrection, the apparent instability of the poem as inscription and/or elegy. Such an instability may confuse the reader. But, as the foregoing remarks have attempted to show, given the nature of the poem the conceitful result of such an instability and complexity is precisely the most productive rhetorical basis of Góngora's objective, Baroque poetry.

IV *An Example of Overlapping Patterns in the Sonnet*

Our next sonnet is also characterized by the instability of reference. Ostensibly an inscription, it too is essentially the elegy of the painter El Greco, and, as such, is based on the same procedure of shifting points of reference, of ambiguous symbolic meanings, as the poem on Margarita's catafalque. We are dealing with a sonnet written only three years later, in 1614:

INSCRIPCIÓN PARA EL SEPULCRO DE DOMINICO GRECO

Esta en forma elegante, oh peregrino
de pórfido luciente dura llave
el pincel niega al mundo más süave,
que dió espíritu a leño, vida a lino.
5 *Su nombre, aun de mayor aliento dino*
que en los clarines de la Fama cabe,
el campo ilustra de ese mármol grave:
venéralo y prosigue tu camino.
Yace el Griego. Heredó Naturaleza
10 *arte; y el Arte estudio, Iris colores.*
Febo luces si no sombras Morfeo.
Tanta urna, a pesar de su dureza
lágrimas beba, y cuantos suda olores
corteza funeral de árbol sabeo.[28]

(INSCRIPTION FOR THE SEPULCHER OF DOMINICO GRECO. This hard key in elegant form, oh pilgrim, of shining porphyry denies to the world the softest brush, which gave spirit to wood, life to linen. His name, worthy of even greater breath than fits in the trumpets of Fame, illuminates the field of that solemn marble: venerate it and continue on your way. Here lies the Greek. Nature inherited Art; and Art, skill; Iris, colors. Phoebus, lights; if not shadows, Morpheus. Let so much urn, despite its hardness, drink tears and whatever fragrances the funeral bark of the Sabaean trees sweats.[29])

Dominico Theotocopuli, *El Greco,* who died in 1614, can certainly be called an epitome of the Spanish Baroque in the realm of painting, and it is therefore not unexpected to find among Góngora's occasional sonnets one devoted to the Greek who contributed so much to the flowering of Spanish art in the seventeenth century. Like the preceding sonnet on the catafalque in Córdoba in honor of Queen Margarita, this sonnet likewise serves the double function of being an "inscription" for the actual physical monument, El Greco's sepulcher, as well as constituting an extravagant elegy. As we shall see, the latter focus of the poem is double in turn, being approximately elegiastic in its very existence, but offering as well a particularly audacious assessment of the significance of such major creative talents as El Greco. As verbal art, the composition is quite complex, both in the syntax of the stanzas and in the meaning of the various segments.

For example, the two quatrains, which do constitute the traditional initial, autonomous unit of the sonnet, contain at least two superimposed syntactic patterns, a feature which may not necessarily be uniquely Baroque, but which is easily attributable to the rhetorical ideals of seventeenth-century writers such as Góngora. One of the two patterns consists of the period opening with the demonstrative *Esta,* whose main noun constituent is contained in the next verse, *dura llave,* with the main verb of the sentence and its inverted direct object in the third verse, *el pincel niega.* The function of this period is to express an attitude toward the sepulcher in which El Greco is entombed. As was the case with Margarita, there is by implication a somewhat hesitant acceptance of the fact of death, represented metonymically by the tomb itself. Thus, Góngora spoke of how the Queen's catafalque was in fact a new Phoenix pyre, from which she would rise again in renewed, supposedly epitomic Christian, glory. In the case of El Greco, the poet laments how the "harsh key" (an oblique reference perhaps to the keys of St. Peter and their ability to bind and to loose?) that is the sepulcher, has denied to the world the brush, which is in turn a metonymy for the poet and his talent, best represented by the symbolic tool. The period up to this point is a web of hyperbatons. One can even question the role of *süave* at the end of line 3. It is a singular adjective and occurs immediately after the singular noun, *mundo.* But does it modify *mundo;* or, more likely, does it modify *pincel,* which occurs a few words back at the beginning of the verse?

In either case, the modification is figurative. If it is of *mundo,* we would imagine a select world of taste, to which both the artist and the poet would count themselves as belonging. This is not altogether improbable, since the Baroque artist saw himself as the member of a blessed elite far removed from the *vulgo,* the crude and untutored masses; and Góngora himself had much to say in his letters about his alliance with such a belief. If, on the other hand, the modification is of the painter's brush, *süave* surely could not refer to any physical property, but to the elegance of talent with which El Greco's hand manipulated the tool. Although one might find some reference to this sort of ambiguous displacement of adjectival modifiers in Uhrhan's purely linguistic analysis of Góngora's syntax,[30] I know of no study examining with reference to artistic issues this all too frequent phenomenon of Góngora's style, although Dámaso Alonso has addressed himself on several occasions to examples of hyperbaton.[31] While in the final analysis one is likely to attribute the adjective *süave* to *pincel* rather than to *mundo,* its very displacement is disconcerting to an initial, superficial reading and demonstrates the extent to which the reader is forced to pay unusual attention to matters which, in colloquial, nonpoetic discourse, are routine syntax.

From another point of view, the critic announces, of course, that this is precisely one of the goals of such violations of routine syntax (another goal being the much touted attempts to imitate Greek and Latin syntax). Note also the conclusion of this initial period in the final line of the quatrain. Verse 4 is an appositional clause of *pincel* (this is an interpretive assertion, since the syntax is not explicit as regards the antecedent of the relative pronoun *que* and there are six singular nouns altogether in the first three lines to which, in theory, the relative pronoun plus its singular verb could refer). What is important, however, is not an ambiguity of antecedent, but the structure of the two direct objects of the verb of the clause, *dió.* Both are identical in structure (noun [direct object]-preposition-noun [indirect object]) and are joined, not by the usual conjuction, but by an asyndetic comma. The second phrase, "life to canvas," is appropriate to the activity of the artist's brush, but the first phrase, "spirit to wood," is rather vague in its meaning, since El Greco is known neither as a sculptor in wood (which would not be accomplished via the brush in the first place) nor as a painter of the wooden triptychs of an earlier, medieval era. Of course, the references are quite metaphoric to begin with (although the giving in art of "spirit" and "life" to the object is readily understood), and one is on dangerous critical ground to insist, as John Crowe Ransom once tried in the case of Shakespeare's sonnets, that there be any logical correlation between language and referent.[32]

The sentence of the second quatrain is really an extension of the first sentence which we have been discussing and belongs also to the first of the two superimposed patterns. Again, there is superficially a violation of logic, since, seen in isolation, there is little question that *su nombre* is to be understood as "his (El Greco's) name," and the quatrain goes on to speak hyperbolically of its deserving even greater trumpeting than that which Fame's clarions can give it and of its giving luster to the noble marble of the sepulcher itself. But when read together with the first quatrain, logic is indeed violated, since, ostensibly, *su* refers to *pincel,* the painter's brush. Of course, upon closer examination the reader is to realize that the brush is, as we have stated, a metonymy for the man himself whose name is at issue in the following stanza, but the superficial semantic conflict between the two nouns "brush" and "name," which are tied together syntactically by the third-person possessive, is yet another example of the extreme fluidity of quotidian logic and linguistic expression that is so disconcerting to the casual reader of Góngora's poetry. A brief linguistic excursus: note that in the translation of *su nombre* English must make an interpretational decision, since possessive pronouns in English agree with the gender and number of the person who possesses. The Spanish *su,* on the other hand, is simply third-person singular, and therefore may refer to a possessor which is biologically masculine, feminine or neither (i.e., "its"). Thus the Spanish phrase is simply vague as to the immediate antecedent of *su nombre,* while an English translation must specify either "its name" and therefore refer to the brush itself, or "his name" and thereby refer to the true metonymic meaning of brush—El Greco himself.

The second period superimposed upon the statement descriptive of the artist's tomb is a vocative to the pilgrim, the *oh peregrino* of the second half of the first verse. The main verb and other predicate elements of this subject are to be found in the concluding line of the second stanza. Thus the entire sentence, consisting of only seven words, is a frame for the first segment of the sonnet, since it is contained in only the initial and final verses of the unit formed by the two quatrains. The main verb of this vocative is an imperative and commands the pilgrim to venerate the sepulcher before continuing on his way. Why the reference is to a pilgrim rather than simply any traveler or other second person is not immediately evident. Góngora has several sonnets, serious and otherwise, which contain such vocatives to the pilgrim traveler. But here one can justify the necessity of the second person being a pilgrim by the overall rhetorical attitude toward the sepulcher. It is not that the poem is addressed to anyone who happens to be a pilgrim, but that anyone who happens to contemplate El Greco's sepulcher must consider himself a pilgrim by virtue of the pseudoreligious stature of the artist. His tomb is to be considered virtually a shrine, to be accorded all of the respect and veneration of a holy place—hence the imperative verb that begins line 8: "venerate it" (the pronoun, masculine, nonhuman and singular, probably refers to *pórfido,* "porphyry," line 2). Thus, the function of the superimposed periods—the first consisting of two sentences, one for each of the two quatrains, and the second consisting of the short vocative—is to highlight an attitude toward El Greco and his funeral monument. It would have been possible for the poet simply to describe the sepulcher in hyperbolic terms, and this he effectively does with reference to how the "harsh key" denies the brush to the world or to how Fame's clarions are inadequate to the task of proclaiming the man's virtues. But by superimposing on these references the vocative to a putative observer who must assume the humble stance of the pilgrim in veneration of the holy shrine, Góngora, on a quite distinct rhetorical level, implies with noteworthy subtlety a further hyperbolic assessment of the importance of El Greco. That Góngora makes use of a religious allusion, given profane meaning, to speak of El Greco's importance should not be taken as any personal religious flippancy on Góngora's part, despite whatever corroboration one might in fact find in the details of his rather lax priestly career. The tradition of the profaned religious hyperbole is deeply rooted in a Spanish tradition which is so thoroughly institutionally Catholic that incidental accommodations of religious phrases, symbols, litanies, etc., to distinctly profane contexts can be tolerated without any meaningful threat to proper reverence.[33]

Much more audacious in terms of accepted beliefs is the form of the hyperbole of praise to El Greco's artistic talents in the first tercet of the sonnet. Leaving aside the totally unexpected initial three-word sentence, "Here lies El Greco," which must settle at the bottom of any statistical listing of the poet's preferences in sentence length, the reader's attention is most called to the series of equally brief statements that occupy the rest of the stanza. (Their semantic interrelationship leaves the impression of one compound period, which is indeed the way in which our text is punctuated, although some texts posit at least three distinct sentences.) What is striking and startling about what is stated is the reversal of the accepted relationship between Nature and Art. Throughout the Renaissance, and stretching back to classical concepts of artistic mimesis, one finds a consistent belief in the role of the artist as an imitator of nature in one way or another. Thus, as Arthur Terry has argued,[34] although the Baroque theory of art modifies somewhat the basis of that imitation toward a more creative, ingenious, "conceitful" reflection of universal Nature, there still remains the belief that the poet is, in the last analysis, portraying an idealized Nature and its underlying universals (as opposed to the particulars of a specific historico-biographical time and place that one finds in some major versions of Romantic-modern literature). While Nature may on occasion identify with the joy or with the sufferings of man (cf. Garcilaso de la Vega's *First Eclogue*)—the poetic license of pathetic fallacy—it is still the practice for art to portray nature, as we find in Garcilaso's other major composition, the *Third Eclogue*, where the water nymphs weave a rich tapestry—as does the poem itself—that portrays, via materials taken from Nature itself, several stories of amorous suffering and tragedy. But here, Góngora, in his desire to express as succinctly and as conceitfully as possible the esteem in which El Greco must properly be held, in his desire to provide figuratively an appropriate emblematic inscription for the painter's sepulcher, inverts this relationship.[35] Thus Nature, rather than inspiring the artist, is inspired by him. Paradigmatic references concerning the artist's inspiration—such as Iris, from whom the artist takes his colors; Phoebus Apollo, from whom his brilliance—are now to take their qualities from the artist himself.

The use of the verb "inherited" in line 9 refers to the artist's death, to his return to Nature. Somewhat pantheistically, his talents in death have been distributed among those elements of Nature that normally make art possible: this may be a rather conceitful and abstract restatement of the orthodox Christian formula of man's physical return to the dust from which he came, although spiritual qualities are certainly implied by El Greco's "return" to Nature. This is not Góngora's first inversion of the relationship Nature-man, since in the first sonnet which we discussed we saw how the beauty of the woman was such as to put various fundamental manifestations of Nature to shame. But this is the most audacious and the most direct affirmation of this type of hyperbolic inversion of what was considered to be a normal relationship between Nature and the artist, and it is quite effective, if one understands its point of departure in routine Renaissance art theory, in bespeaking the supreme talents of El Greco. One last note on this point: it is stated that Nature has inherited Art. By the latter noun is meant, we assume, El Greco in an eponymic sense: he is Art personified, and thus Art, which was once inspired by Nature, has returned to Nature to serve as her inspiration.

Given the characteristics of the quatrains and the first tercet, the final stanza of the sonnet is distinctly anticlimactic and merits attention only for the complexity of its syntax. Although some attention might be paid to the phrasing of the allusion to the trees of Saba or Sheba and the rightful incense for the sepulcher to which they refer, it is the syntax that is more problematical. The subject, *tanta urna,* goes with the subjunctive verb *beba,* which constitutes therefore an indirect command. Symmetrically, the main verb is flanked by two direct objects, *lágrimas* and *olores,* although the latter object is preceded by the relative particle *cuantos* that introduces the appositional clause that defines it. Perhaps one could see a correlation between this double direct object and the two objects of *dió* in line 4. Certainly in the latter case the reference is to the product of the artist's talent and in the last stanza the reference is to what recognition the death of such a talent is to evoke. But we can see no semantic basis to solidify such a correlation; once again, it may be the sort of casual bringing together of essentially unrelated elements that we spoke of with reference to the last line of the sonnet "Mientras por competir con tu cabello." Certainly, the network of syntactic and semantic patterns of the sonnet on El Greco—both elegy and emblematic eulogy—is complex enough without insisting on any such correlation that would tie the final stanza in with the opening one.

V *Conclusions*

Stephen Booth, in concluding one section of his exhaustive study of poetic structure in the sonnets of William Shakespeare, makes the following observations apropos of the rhetorical and formal complexities of the individual compositions:

> One of my purposes in this essay is to support the thesis that in all their details the sonnets set a reader's mind in motion, demand intellectual energy as they are read, and that that effect of the actual experience of passing from word to word for fourteen lines, is unusual and valuable. Each reading of a Shakespeare sonnet is a peculiarly real experience for its reader. It is the experience not of recognizing the mutable nature of the human condition but of participating in an actual experience of mutability.
>
> As he reads a Shakespeare sonnet, a reader's mind moves from one system of relationship to another just as it does when it contemplates physical experience. [. . . In] the sonnets where the experience of imperceptible shifting is both scaled down to a size appropriate to the sixty-second experience of reading a fourteen-line poem, and exaggerated by the concentration and diversity of its manifestations, a reader's mind is constantly moving from one scheme to another in its perceptions of verse units, syntactical units, sound patterns, image patterns, and the relationships of word to word, object to object, person to person, and idea to idea in the course of reading a poem.[36]

Whether or not Shakespeare is appropriately labelled Baroque is really beside the point.[37] Speaking either from the limited perspective of Góngora and Shakespeare as contemporaries who necessarily partook of European literary currents that converged in many fundamental ways or from the broader perspective of the very nature of poetry as a typically dense form of literary expression, it should be apparent that much of what Booth has to say is equally applicable to the sonnets of Góngora as we have discussed them in this chapter.

Although we have had the space to deal with only four of Góngora's 166 sonnets,[38] we have been able to discuss these four in some detail precisely in order to demonstrate adequately both their complexity and originality of structure. It should be apparent from our comments that these sonnets, like Shakespeare's—and like all poetry, Baroque or otherwise, and to one degree or another—reveal a pattern of form, and therefore of meaning, that is not simply the linear order of the words themselves, despite the fact that we have excluded a discussion of many of the aspects of structure of the individual compositions that could, in a more exhaustive presentation, be taken up, such as phonological and lexical patterns. Several times in passing we have insisted on the objective nature of these sonnets. Aside from the theoretical question of whether Góngora's sonnets do in fact constitute "objective structures" any more than, say, do Garcilaso de la Vega's sonnets (or Santillana's, for that matter, to go back to the first sonneteer in Spanish[39]), our insistence can at least be said to fulfill a practical function of focusing attention on how this literature demands, in its artistic self-consciousness, an overwhelming attention to formal questions.

Robert Jammes may well be just in arguing that, from a purely thematic point of view, Góngora's courtly poetry is essentially unoriginal and that his importance must rest on the iconoclastic *Weltanschauung* of those satirical and other works that reject a prevalent social and aesthetic value system. This may be true, from a purely thematic point of view. But we have wanted, as somewhat of a counterbalance to the "neocontent" orientation of Jammes's impressively thorough study to maintain that, whatever the originality of the raw poetic material may be, the sonnets deserve attention, first for any singularity of poetic structure, and second, for whatever ways in which uniqueness of structure may project upon the raw poetic material a corresponding uniqueness of context. We would also insist, as a further validation for this approach to Góngora's poetry, that such a critical orientation is arguably that much more valid in the case of a Baroque aesthetic—*culteranista* or whatever—that is, as we have already said, artistically self-conscious to an enormous degree.

CHAPTER 4

El Polifemo

I *Introduction*

THE cornerstones of Góngora's poetic fame—and the major foci of the controversies which have surrounded his work from the time of his first compositions—are the two long narrative poems, *El Polifemo (Polyphemus)* and *Las soledades (The Solitudes)*. Both date from the early part of the second decade of the seventeenth century, the former having probably been composed in 1612 and the first part of the latter in 1613; publication of the texts dates from 1613 and 1614, respectively. Both are narrative or pseudo-narrative in nature: the *Polyphemus* is a retelling, with significant touches of originality, of the classical myth as it was widely known by the Renaissance through Ovid's *Metamorphoses*, Chapter 13, verses 750–897; the *Solitudes* are only loosely narrative and recount the episodic bucolic encounters of a shipwrecked pilgrim (see the following chapter). Both works were widely acclaimed in their time as well as widely denounced for roughly the same reasons: the confusion of genres, a distinction between which the Renaissance theoreticians had sought to reestablish after the relative chaos of medieval literary theory; the dense originality of expressive language, both in the area of vocabulary and syntax *(culteranismo)* as well as in the area of complex figures of thoughts, metaphors, conceits, allusions, etc. *(conceptismo)*[1]; the lack of a clear distinction between the lyrical and the narrative, and so on. In short, the discussions generally have involved an appropriate estimation of the poet's originality in these works. For his admirers, the very fact that these two compositions represented such a radical departure from established Renaissance poetic traditions constituted an originality of the highest literary merit: Góngora's supporters were able to see the ways in which his works represented a totally innovative and vanguardistic interpretation of poetic mimesis. On the other hand, the detractors were quite simply unable to accept such audacious departures from what were becoming hallowed theoretical conventions in the understanding of mimesis, literary language, and genre.

Although the detractors triumphed in one sense—the extent to which their dogmatism eventually came to dominate in the neoclassicism of the eighteenth century, a time when Góngora was universally scorned—modern reevaluations of his work have focused on the two long compositions as indicative, precisely, of the genius of his poetic accomplishments which are both paradigmatic and symbolic of the ultimate successes of Spanish Renaissance and Baroque poetry.[2] The reevaluation of Góngora's work, as we have already pointed out in the first chapter of this study, dates basically from the mid-twenties in Spain, and the contributions of Dámaso Alonso, the major critical voice of the generation, have been immense in restoring a balanced perspective on the Cordoban's work. Although first published in 1930, Walter Pabst's comments on the two works, indicative of the reassessment of the Baroque which was taking place elsewhere in Europe, in this case Germany, serves as a valuable summary of the general current critical position via-à-vis Góngora's two major compositions: the dedication of an overall study of Góngora's poetic art to these two compositions, rather than to the complete works, stresses the degree to which the *Polyphemus* and the *Solitudes* early came to be considered the key to his entire literary production. Moreover, one of the most complete studies ever devoted to a Spanish literary text is Dámaso Alonso's commentary—an extended *explication de texte*—on the *Polyphemus,* now in its fifth edition. Alonso's minute examination of the text stresses once again the underlying belief that the *Polyphemus* can be used as a point of departure not only for Góngora's poetry, but more importantly for the Spanish Baroque as a whole.

At the same time, Alonso's edition bespeaks his belief, which, it should be observed, we tend to subscribe to, that the *Polyphemus* is, when the balance sheet has been struck, the most perfect literary composition produced by Góngora. Although the *Solitudes* are perhaps somewhat more innovational—one might want to insist on the greater originality of eschewing completely any dependence on classical literary models, such as the myth of Polyphemus, and of effecting more completely a fusion of narrative and lyrical genres—the *Solitudes* represent an unfinished work, Góngora having completed only the first of four projected parts and somewhat more than half of the second. Thus, whatever else may be said about the two works, the *Polyphemus* represents more of a complete, organic whole than the *Solitudes,* which can never be understood as a unified poem. This circumstance will not bother most readers and critics, but will nevertheless continue to prejudice any assessment based on formal, intrinsic criteria. At the same time, given the perfection of the *Polyphemus* and its chronological standing before the *Solitudes* with their even greater, if incomplete, innovative originality, there has been the tendency to see the former only in terms of a prefigurement of the latter composition. Thus, while Robert Jammes accords the work its due as great poetry, he devotes only half the space to it that is devoted to the latter work, and stresses those elements of the *Polyphemus* which mark the transition in Góngora's poetry from more traditional Renaissance forms to the totally original conception of the *Solitudes.*[3]

But then this has always been the inherent danger of a strictly chronological conception of an artist's work, and in all fairness one must point out that Jammes elsewhere in his study is careful to show a persistent fluctuation in the poet's work between adherence to accepted themes and forms (the amorous sonnets) and a deviation from accepted norms in his poetry which was antiestablishment in both form (the *Solitudes,* the dramas) and theme (satirico-burlesque observations on traditional values, the depiction of the humbly bucolic via a new *stylus gravis* as in the *Solitudes*—this latter facet certainly one of the most disconcerting to the tradition-minded critics). It is simply that the *Polyphemus* to a large extent does represent a transitional bridge, not between an earlier phase and a later, more mature one of the *Solitudes,* but a bridge between traditional forms (the use of myth and a standard narrative form, the *octavas reales*—"royal octaves") and the tremendous liberty with language and structure which is the poet's most abiding contribution. To a large extent, both the *Solitudes* and the *Polyphemus* represent a culmination of the dual reaction of the Baroque, so often found in Góngora's satirical and cynical poetry, against both a pseudosophisticated court *and* the artificiality of the hackneyed, Vergilian-bucolic alternative, such as we find in the pastoral works of Montemayor or Gil Polo, Lope de Vega or Cervantes. The countryside of the former work is the more verisimilar world of the humble peasant rather than the nobleman playing at shepherd, while the "classic" setting of the *Polyphemus* (Sicily) is superficially standard pastoral, only to be shattered by the terrible dark forces of Nature/human nature as personified by the enraged Polyphemus. In both cases, then, the world of Góngora's two major compositions is one which is quite unrecognizable in terms of the pastoral commonplaces of his age. Indeed, one might argue convincingly that the *Polyphemus* is all the more effective precisely to the extent that it uses as a point of departure a widely accepted setting—the story of Polyphemus and Galatea had already had wide treatment in both Spanish and European literature thanks to the continued vitality of Ovid's influence—only to show the destruction of that idyll when it comes under the shadow of the true forces of that primordial human experience, sexual passion. This is an ultimate form of pathetic fallacy, which far exceeds the customary limits of rocks and trees which weep and sigh with the disappointed lover.

II *Treatment of Ovid's Myth*

Góngora's treatment of the Ovidian story is in some ways basically a retelling of traditional material, although there are also several significant innovations.[4] For one thing, Ovid restricted himself to 160 lines of poetry; Góngora needs some five hundred, divided into sixty-three stanzas of eight lines each. The Spanish version, whose complete title is *Fábula de Polifemo y Galatea (The Fable of. . .)*, consists of a three-stanza introduction-dedication and three major movements, the structure of which is discussed later in this chapter. The first movement describes the Sicilian setting and the monstrous shepherd, Polyphemus, and his love for Galatea, the sea nymph. As in Ovid's poem, some space is devoted both to Polyphemus' physical appearance, as well as to his material possessions, possessions which on the one hand are meant to symbolize the bucolic ideal, and on the other to be used to win the beautiful Galatea. The second movement, which, as Jammes has pointed out in some detail, represents a significant contribution by Góngora to the legend, focuses on the love between Galatea and Acis; to this extent it represents a counterpoint to the first movement, as we see Galatea become the beloved, not of Polyphemus, but of Acis. Góngora devotes considerable space to detailing the awakening of passion between Galatea and Acis, and his concentration on the erotic constitutes a valuable advancement over earlier treatments of the encounter. At the same time, the space devoted to the lyrical evocation of the encounter, an evocation which is accorded all the poet's powers of invention so that it becomes one extended and complex conceit, is a departure from the purely narrative mode that one would expect to dominate in the retelling of a classical myth. To be sure, this is not original with Góngora in this poem, for we have seen how in the ballad on Angélica and Medoro, composed at about the same time, the strictly narrative presentation of the coming together of the fates of the two individuals is overlain by an intensely lyrical evocation of the love which blossoms between them. The third movement or segment of the poem is the denouement, and relates how Polyphemus discovers the love bower of the two and in his rage destroys Acis by crushing him with a boulder; the poem moves very rapidly toward a conclusion with only the briefest mention of Acis' metamorphosis into a river, thus departing again from Ovid, who, as one would expect, concentrates great attention on the transformation itself.

Looking back over the preceding summary of the poem's "plot," one is tempted almost to speak in dramatic terms of a three-act partition (the basic form of the Lopesque *comedia*) into representation (Polyphemus, his setting, and his love), complication (Galatea's love for Acis, rather than for Polyphemus), resolution (the protagonist's elimination of his rival, Acis, and the immortalization of the latter by Galatea through the metamorphosis). While Góngora appeared to have an aversion to Lope's conception of dramatic structure (cf. his Aristotelian play *The Constancy of Isabela*), the *Polyphemus* does bear a striking resemblance to such a tripartite division, which is enhanced precisely by the poet's fleshing out of the pivotal encounter between Galatea and the unsuspecting Acis (Galatea, of course, in being pursued not only by Polyphemus but also by various sea gods and shepherds and, in thus bringing Acis to his unsuspected doom because of her beauty, is somewhat of a *femme fatale, avant la lettre*). In any case, a close reading of Góngora's text reveals a striking shift in focus from earlier Renaissance treatments of the material, and, although he is making use of stock mythological material, there can be little doubt that in line with the best of literary imitation during the Renaissance, his is a totally creative work, unlike many preceding treatments that can be called little more than loose translations of Ovid's text. As we shall discuss in a moment, what is more significant is Góngora's attitude toward his material and the subsequent fashion in which he reinterprets the legend in terms of his own personal conception of human experience. From the purely external point of view of thematic elaboration, we have mentioned how Góngora modifies his material in the two significant ways of expanding the erotic encounter between Galatea and Acis and, conversely, of downplaying the metamorphosis itself. In addition to these two changes, one may note, as Jammes has stressed, a certain tendency on Góngora's part to humanize Polyphemus. No longer is he just the enraged monster of traditional mythology, but, despite his physical appearance, he takes on very definite human emotional attributes, and herein lies one of the most significant alterations by the poet of his material. There will be more on this aspect as we proceed with our analysis of the poem.

III *Some Critical Problems*

As background to a careful consideration of the text itself, it is necessary to dwell on several problems presented by the *Polyphemus.* Given Góngora's work as a whole and his general iconoclastic stance toward literary tradition, particularly in his most important compositions, one is immediately struck by his use of a traditional myth. While it is true that he makes the material creatively his own and that one can in no way speak of mere "literary imitation" (Pabst, among others, put that vacuous charge to rest), his use of the Polyphemus material is nevertheless somewhat curious, and his only other extensive use of mythological material is to satirize (as he did with the story of Leander and Hero on several occasions).[5] To put the problem in a sharper persepctive we might ask, quite directly, what did Góngora mean to portray by his reworking of the story of Polyphemus? His must be much more than mere poetic exercise, which was often the case with the commonplace reworking in the Renaissance of material from Ovid and other mythological sources. The *Polyphemus* must be seen as something more than a decorative poem, although the earlier discussions of the work by the 1927 generation of poets in Spain, who are credited in great part with Góngora's "resurrection," tended to focus on brilliant but therefore only isolated examples of expressive perfection in his poetry; little interest emerges either in discussing the overall structure of the poem (and this holds especially true of the *Solitudes*) or in providing the general outlines of a satisfactory interpretation capable of demonstrating the deep human concerns of the poet.

Dámaso Alonso, who, it should be evident, has done the most to provide the scholar and general reader with a coherent body of critical guidelines, has underlined the conflict in the poem between beauty and monstrosity—sort of a pre-Romantic clash between "the Beauty and the Beast."[6] This conflict, which may be seen in terms of Polyphemus' relationship to both ideal lovers, Galatea as well as Acis, Alonso insists repeatedly on seeing as the quintessence of Góngora's *Weltanschauung*. Certainly seen in these terms, the poem can be rather effortlessly seen to bring into play not only the integrating forces of the universe which tended to be the "image" of Medieval and Renaissance humanists,[7] but also the disintegrating forces which, although they are never far below the surface in pre-Baroque European thought, seem, until the seventeenth century, to be more overwhelmed by man's faith in an essentially universal transcendency of nature and human emotions. Although it would be easy to accuse this line of discussion as simplistic vis-à-vis the complexities of Renaissance thought, the Spanish Baroque, at least, is well known for its preoccupations with the multifaceted threats to man's emotional as well as his psychological tranquility. And the lack of any implicit consolation for Góngora in the reaffirmation of Counter-Reformation Catholicism to be found in Lope de Vega or Calderón de la Barca makes all that more stark those elements in his work which underline cynically, sarcastically, ironically the fundamental instability of human ideals.[8]

Although some case can be made for backgrounds representative of a strain of Renaissance Neoplatonism,[9] there has been, we feel, greater critical success in approaching the *Polyphemus* along lines less explicitly identified with specific intellectual or thematic issues. What has emerged from general discussions of Góngora by Collard and from specific observations on the *Polyphemus* by Smith[10] and by Jammes (despite the brevity of the latter's comments) is an insight into the peculiar effect produced by the amoral cosmos of the poem and by the poet's attitude toward his material which tends to bring Polyphemus and the two lovers together on a more unified emotional level than that represented by the antithesis between beauty and monstrosity, which Jammes, rightly so, feels has been far overemphasized by Alonso and his followers. Jammes discusses with some conviction the manner in which the legendary cyclops is given an essential humanity by Góngora. The French critic does not address himself to the question of why the poet would be interested in so modifying Polyphemus' character, although there can be little question that it is, most decidedly, not out of any prefiguratively Romantic desire, à la Grimm and Mrs. Shelley, to sentimentalize the monster. While we still are obliged to demonstrate our declarations with close reference to the text itself, we propose, as a preliminary understanding of Góngora's attitude toward his characters, that the poet is only pursuing his recurring interest in understanding the basic principles of human nature. One version of that understanding is to focus on the "monstrous" aspects of the human being, a focusing which unquestionably comes through in his satiric and scatological poetry. But what better way to emphasize the hitherto unheard-of, because so blatantly anti-Christian, interrelationship between the human and the amorally monstrous than by taking a paradigmatic figure of the monstrous and turning him into another human figure who comes brutally up against the reality of love and passion? Thus the essential conflict of the poem is not over a pair of human lovers whose idyll is destroyed by blind and vengeful forces of an uncomprehending nature, but rather the inevitable disaster and tragedy which can be the only result of intensely-felt human passions, in this case the all-too-human passion of Polyphemus for the aloof Galatea. The former's hideous rage and its consequences are, one cannot fail to note, parallel to those of Count Roland which are so effectively introduced at the conclusion of the ballad of Angélica and Medoro as the inevitable human reality of their passionate idyll. Although in the ballad, written approximately at the same time as the *Polyphemus*, the enraged Count never actually appears, there can be little doubt from the poet's dramatic conclusion that those lovers are threatened by unchecked forces of jealous human passion which come to be given full play in the longer composition (see above, pp. 38–47).

It has been noted that in Góngora's version little attention is paid the metamorphosis of Acis, which was, after all, the motivating interest of Ovid's original version. Góngora's emphasis, again reminiscent of the ballad, is in adding a detailing of the idyll of the two lovers and thereby bringing out that much more effectively the collision course between that idyllic love and the dark human emotions which it awakens in the cyclops. Andrée Collard is one of the recent scholars who have spoken in general terms of Góngora's amoral world, and Smith's article provides much reinforcement from the *Polyphemus* alone. Although the latter critic could be accused of unfortunate anachronism in speaking of the "Darwinian" world of the *Polyphemus*, it would be hard to disagree with the main outlines of his study:

> . . . The *Polifemo* as a result has a large and serious theme: the world of Nature and man's place in it. The poem is about unity and disruption, harmony and discord, light and dark, nature cruel and nature kind, nature untamed and nature productive, masculine and feminine, violence and tenderness . . . (p. 220)
>
> The idea of evil is, in fact, necessary to complete the picture of Nature, for no amount of mere prettiness would satisfy us. The idea of violence and death is the last link in the chain of life. There is not merely a visual oneness about Góngora's Nature, but a logic in its functioning which conveys a sense of almost Darwinian completeness. The origins of life are not known scientifically but are explained in fragile fictions, which can then be further glossed in a poetic way exactly suited to Góngora's art. (p. 230)

What Smith is getting at, if we understand him correctly, is that the world of the poem is essentially deterministic: on one level are individuals who live out an existence in direct and telluric contact with nature; but on another and higher level, their emotions and their life cycle is an enactment of the entire drama of Nature itself, which, because it is a drama ruled by unknown and unalterable forces, is inescapably amoral. Thus it would be impertinent to question the morality of Polyphemus' actions—or, for that matter, of Galatea's aloofness (like Angélica's) before the sincerity of her suitors, until melted by a blinding vision of masculine beauty (note, again, the parallel of Acis with Medoro). Indeed, and the commentaries on the poem have not stressed this circumstance sufficiently, we feel, the very amorality of the world of the poem and the integration of this overall tone with the theme provide us with precisely an understanding of the unusually forceful impact which it is noted to have on readers, an impact which explains in great part the attention which it has received as typical both of Góngora's Baroque art as well as his fundamental brilliance as a poet. The working out of the deep human passions in the poem, from the uncontrollable blind love between Acis and Galatea to the uncontrollable blind rage in Polyphemus with absolutely no moral condescension on the part of the narrative voice produces in the reader an intense cathartic effect when the idyll of the two lovers is finally so brutally, but "naturally," destroyed. The concluding stanza—the scant eight lines devoted to the metamorphosis of Acis—is a release from that catharsis, as the transformed Apollo figure returns to nature, as a river befitting Galatea's background as a sea nymph, thus concluding with the poem the life cycle of a human being. That it is a life cycle completed via terrible and monstrous forces of human emotion only serves to underline conclusively the amalgam in the poem between a particular conception of nature and man's place in it (Smith), an essentially amoral stance in the face of human nature and passion (Collard), and a cathartic effect meant to engage the reader in an intuitive commitment to the poet's own personal vision of reality. It is in this way that we may speak of the *Polyphemus* as a work which jibes with essential human truths, Baroque or otherwise.

It is in terms of the foregoing comments that we must understand how Polyphemus dominates Góngora's version of the legend, not as a monster, a freak of Nature which therefore must destroy the Nature into whose scheme of idealized beauty he does not fit, but as a particularly stunning and vivid embodiment of one aspect of Nature and, as a consequence, of one most inescapable dark facet of the human soul. Whether one sees the interrelationship between Polyphemus and the lovers as one of an integration of the forces of nature (Smith) or as the tenuousness of idealized human emotion in the face of the inescapable reality of human emotions (our inclination and the basis of our references to the *Romance of Angélica and Medoro*), one must come back time and again to the realization that Góngora's Polyphemus is endowed with far greater symbolic emotions than the monster of Ovid's story or of his sixteenth-century imitators. Of course Góngora is interested in his character's monstrosity; if he were not it would be absurd for him to have chosen to retell Ovid's story. That he does, in fact, retell one well-known story is significant to the extent that the educated reader can compare Polyphemus with the original and draw significant conclusions from the change in his nature at Góngora's hands. Although such a philological approach can be an aid to interpretation, the humanized characteristics of the cyclops, assumedly recognizable on the basis of the text alone, should be sufficient to alert the reader and to cause him to raise the question as to why this fashion of juxtaposing the dreadful collision of two blind passions, a collision which, because of the absolute amoral vacuum of Góngora's poetic universe, assumes almost tragic proportions. As Lowry Nelson has observed, through his revealing analysis of the uncertainty of verbal tense in the narrative, the overall effect is one of a timeless circumstance, of an inalterable pattern of events: "the reader is left at the end of the 'Polifemo' with no guarantee that the same action will not happen again or does not happen repeatedly."[11] Such a conclusion is indicative of a poetry which may be a form of pure verbal brilliance, but one which nevertheless bespeaks with tremendous emotional impact for the reader some profound intuitions concerning the nature of human experience and emotion.

What has gone before is the barest outline of an adequate discussion of the *Polyphemus*. For the reader unfamiliar with the text, there cannot help but be the impression of a rather belabored series of generalizations. Nevertheless, since we are unable to quote the entire poem and to analyze all of its facets line by line, as we did in the case of the shorter compositions, it has been felt indispensable to give some sort of general presentation of the poem and of the difficulties of interpretation and appreciation which it represents as the necessary prelude to the intricacies of the text itself, intricacies the satisfactory characterization of which all too often results in the loss of a sense of the totality of the composition. With some sense of the whole of the work in mind from the foregoing pages, let us now proceed to a concentration on some of the intricacies which understandably have attracted no little critical attention.

IV *Poetic Unity*

Given the extended, narrative nature of the *Polyphemus*, it is impossible to subject it to the sort of extended analysis appropriate for a sonnet. Moreover, if one subscribes, as we do, to the critical assumption that different forms of literature evince different organizing, structural principles, it is all the more apparent that we must proceed with this composition of sixty-three stanzas in quite another fashion than with the fourteen-line sonnets. Obviously, the sonnets, for all the overlapping patterns which they may reveal upon analysis, can with little room for dissent be said to operate on the principle of one unifying motif, conceit, or theme, such as was the case with the underlying conditional, imperative statement of the first sonnet studied in the previous chapter. On the other hand, a longer work, one which can be more properly called narrative than can a sonnet (can a sonnet ever be narrative in any strict sense of the word?), while it may possess a poetic unity based on one simple or complex motif, of necessity contains potentially many different but interrelated threads of organization, many of the latter perhaps only the sort of digressive amplification of subject matter, background material, support for verisimilitude, etc., which we traditionally associate with the narrative in either poetry or prose. We have by way of introduction to the poem made some prefatory statements concerning the nature of the *Polyphemus* and the overall sense of its impact upon the reader. Such statements should be considered a tentative "interpretation" of the poem, against which observations concerning the various parts and techniques of the composition should be compared as we proceed with a more direct consideration of the text itself. This is especially true where we cannot present the reader with a complete text of the poem; for a better understanding, he is advised to consult one, although we shall quote many portions of the text itself in order to demonstrate our assertions.

Despite the continued influence in Spanish scholarship of Wölfflin's art theories concerning the Baroque,[12] particularly as regards the supposed "organic unity" of the latter aesthetic (pre-Baroque Renaissance works are said to evince "multiplicity" or "relative unity"), many critics have observed not only the tripartite movement of the poem, but the independence of the poet's dedicatory opening as well. Consisting of three stanzas, this opening has attracted critical interest on its own, quite apart from questions concerning the main body of the poem.[13] Frattoni examines essentially the texture of the three opening stanzas, while Caldera insists that, more than simply serving the traditional purpose of attracting reader attention and providing the requisite encomium of a patron or potential patron, the three stanzas reflect faithfully all of the thematic and stylistic features of the poem as a whole. This is not a surprising conclusion, since it would be more unexpected were the stanzas disconsonant with the main body of the composition. Certainly all of Góngora's major stylistic effects are here: hyperbaton, hyperbole, conceit, metonymy, synecdoche, correlation (parataxis), allusion, unconventional use of vocabulary or referents (such as the invocation of the classical muse Thalia, associated with comedy, but invoked by Góngora in her all-but-forgotten pastoral role per Vergil and Horace).

More significant than merely surface texture are the two ways in which Góngora uses the introductory stanzas to prelude the underlying premises of his version of Polyphemus and Galatea. In stanza 12, the poet describes, as one of the attributes of the cyclops, his large-scale pipes of Pan, made of a hundred giant reeds. The description of Polyphemus closes with an epiphonema referring to the horrible music that, metonymically, is an extension of the monster and bespeaks his disruption of tranquil nature. Later, in stanza 45, after the poet has described in great detail the secret union of Acis and Galatea in their hidden bower (note the departure from Ovid's version, where from the outset the cyclops knows of the love between the two), Polyphemus, who has been absent from the long parenthesis dealing with Galatea and Acis' union (ss. 13–14), reappears with his pipes to sing a song of love and enticement to the absent Galatea. Stanza 45 too ends with an epiphonema, the only use in the poem of the topos of poetic inability, wherein the poet calls upon the Muses (using their name Pierides) to relate the thunderous cacophony of Polyphemus' music. It is in stanza 45 where the pipes are identified with the noun *zampoña* (English zampogna, related etymologically and ironically to English symphony).

There is a very real importance played by music in the poem, particularly at the juncture of stanza 45, where Polyphemus reappears with all the tumultuous noise of his pipes to interrupt with terrible vengeance the blissful union of Galatea and Acis, a union which, in stanzas 40–44, has been described in terms of a deep silence punctuated only by the gentle cooing of attendant doves (undoubtedly a metaphoric—if not euphemistic—objectification of the private murmurings of passion by the two lovers). But aside from this significant element of the poem's structure, there is a distinct correlation to be made between the references to the cyclops' zampogna and its horrendous sounds, sounds which the poet must ironically appeal to the Muses to describe, and the poet's own music which is the poem itself. Or to put it in other terms, the poet's own song which is the poem, and Polyphemus' song quoted in detail in stanzas 44–58 (almost one-fourth of the total lines of the composition). This correlation is established by the poet's appeal to his patron, the Conde de Niebla, to set aside his hunting gear and to attend to his, the poet's, zampogna (stanza 1) and its verses, dictated by Thalia, the bucolic or pastoral muse. One might claim that this is a relationship too slight to be of any major critical interest: the two references are separated by forty-some stanzas. This however is not a valid comment, since the student of Góngora (to avoid generalizing in terms of all of Baroque poetry) must accustom himself to assessing meanings which are expressed either so laconically as to attract almost no attention, or expressed so conceitfully as to be virtually meaningless (as for example the meaning of the epiphonema which concludes stanza 22 and the description of the effects which Galatea's beauty has on those who pursue her in vain).[14] Moreover, we have seen in our discussion of Góngora's shorter compositions that it is precisely this sort of correlation which reinforces the overall unity of his compositions. In this case, the correlation used implies a necessary correspondence between the poet's consciously created artifice and the "natural" activities of Nature and her elements, the latter Polyphemus' song in this case, even if it is more a disruption of idyllic Nature than a projection of it. The reader will recall that Góngora made an issue of much the same correspondence in his ballad on the pinecone harvesters, discussed at the end of Chapter 2. The "natural" song of one of their own is meant to be compared with the poet's objective composition. Of course, underlying all this is the oft-repeated statement that Baroque art, although in a very fundamental sense it may be a form of mimesis, is the result of the poet's conscious desire to "supplement" Nature by juxtaposing to it or imposing upon it his own creative artifice.

This latter notion is very much at issue in the *Polyphemus* as a whole and, quite aside from the references to the poet's music vs.

the monster's music, which is only a corroborating detail, concerns the way in which the narrative itself is an artful composition imposed upon the natural setting of Sicily. Sicily is there as the necessary background, and Góngora to this extent is simply repeating a detail of his source material. But on one level the terrifying events of the three main characters, Polyphemus, Galatea, and Acis, are imposed upon that setting. It should be viewed as no accident that all three are sea elements which have come upon land, so to speak: Polyphemus is the son of Neptune, Galatea is the daughter of the sea divinity Doris, while Acis is son of a sea nymph and a faun. When Acis is crushed by Polyphemus' rock, he is turned into a crystalline stream which flows back to the sea, a circumstance of no mean mythic importance (in the modern sense of myth) and reminiscent of those myths dealing with the "return,"[15] in this case less a cyclical return than a return to the source of life.

On another, higher level, Góngora's composition is an imposition upon Nature. He implores his patron to abandon the hunt and for all of Nature to become silent and attentive to his song (stanzas 2 and 3): *Y al cuerno, al fin, la cítara suceda* ("and to the cithara at last let the horn give way"[16]). His song will deal with a natural setting, but as the song of the poet it will be superimposed upon that setting, will be creative art, even though his song will in turn contain the "natural" song of Polyphemus, the latter on its own level an imposition upon Nature, which reacts with disruption because of its monstrosity. Thus, both poet and monster are "out of place" in the setting of Sicily. Polyphemus, whether one sees him as an accident of Nature or the product of a malevolent god who placed him upon the island, is nevertheless an integral part of his setting. The poet, on the other hand, creates the unmistakably artificial version of that circumstance. The monster sings from the depths of his troubled being; the poet, from the exercise of his conscious art, and there can be no confusing art with nature. This on at least an abstract level implied by the introduction; on the more concrete level of the text itself and those stanzas dealing with Polyphemus' long composition to Galatea, one will want to note how the only differentiation between what the *cultista* poet sings and what the rustic monster sings is that the latter's verses are set off graphically. But then we have already noted how, despite the juxtaposition between art and Nature in the ballad "En los pinares de Xúcar," the rustic girl's song that is quoted does not differ "realistically" in language from that of the poet.

The Cyclops

The first part of the narrative proper is a presentation of the monster of Nature, Polyphemus. Nine stanzas are involved and take up stanzas 4–12 of the standard editions. Although a wholly unsatisfactory substitute for the text itself, the following schematic presentation of these stanzas is useful for what it shows concerning the poet's organization of his materials:

	Sicily —	stanza 4
	Polyphemus' cave —	5–6
Polyphemus	person —	7–8
	pastoral activities —	9
	pastoral accoutrements —	10–12

One of the first characteristics of Góngora's development of his materials which stands out is the basic, incremental movement from the general to the specific. That is, the first stanza (4) is devoted to an evocation of the island of Sicily, a detail which is given little elaboration here, since it is a *sine qua non,* it would appear, of the lengendary material. (See, however, stanzas 18–19, which describe the agricultural wealth of the island as a transitional introduction to the description of the material offerings with which Galatea's pastoral suitors are able to tempt her, albeit in vain.) The next two stanzas (5–6) are given over to a highly creative presentation of the enormous cavern which is Polyphemus' abode. Not only have we moved from the island in general to one salient segment of the island associated with the monster; the presentation itself foreshadows the characterization of the cyclops himself. On the one hand, the cave is both forbidding and foreboding, a geological phenomenon that is the image of its inhabitant:

caliginoso lecho, el seno obscuro
ser de la negra noche nos lo enseña
infame turba de nocturnas aves,
gimiendo tristes y volando graves. (s. 5e–h)

(the nefarious flock of night birds, gloomily groaning and heavily flying, shows us that it, a caliginous bed, is the dark recess of the black night.)

But more interestingly, Góngora anthropomorphizes his Nature to a very great extent. We are not referring merely to pathetic fallacy or to a sort of profound harmony between man and Nature, as when in the stanzas already alluded to the consummation of the passion between Galatea and Acis is attended by dutiful cooing of doves or when the poet describes in quite hyperbolic terms the shuddering of Nature as Polyphemus casts his shadow upon it, the disruption of the elements when he plays his pipes, and so on. It is more an endowing of Nature, or more exactly, certain phenomena of Nature, with features that are specifically human, such that our contemplation of content moves from persons to natural phenomena with little distinction between what is "really" human and what is not. The result is, of course, an integration of what must be considered only falsely antithetical facets of the greater scheme of Nature. Man, as C. Colin Smith has argued, is seen by Góngora as a wholly integrated or integratable manifestation of Nature. One can show this either by dehumanizing man (which Góngora has often been accused of doing) or by humanizing the supposedly nonhuman facets of Nature, which is what he does to a large extent in the *Polyphemus.* Pathetic fallacy only becomes, within this framework, an incidental support for a much broader point of view. Thus, in moving from the general to the specific, the stanzas of this first movement of the poem do more than simply move from setting to main character. The progression from Sicily to hadean cavern to the inhabitant of that cavern is one natural progression. As Dámaso Alonso has shown, there is a certain tradition that sees an organic relationship between the body of Polyphemus and the triangular-shaped island (the three promontories are his two hands and his oined feet): the island is, in effect, his burial mound. Thus it comes as no surprise that the poet goes on to describe the cave as a yawn; his is more than felicitous imagery:

> *De este, pues, formidable de la tierra*
> *bostezo, el melancólico vacío*
> *a Polifemo, horror de aquella sierra,*
> *bárbara choza es, albergue umbrío* . . . (s.6a–d)

Now, the melancholy emptiness of this fearful yawn of the earth is for Polyphemus, terror of that range, a barbarous hut, shadowy dwelling . . .)

The next six stanzas are concerned with the person of Polyphemus imself. From the point of view of assessing the relationship between him and Nature, of attempting to answer the question whence he and his ability to destroy the perfect beauty and harmony represented by the Venus-Apollo figures Galatea and Acis, the proper appreciation of the foregoing is vital. If it is true that Góngora's ordering of his material is such that the reader is led to see Polyphemus as an integral part of his natural setting (albeit the son of the sea god, Neptune, and therefore more directly linked to the sea than to the land), then here is substantial support for interpreting the monster, not as an external element which comes or is sent to destroy the true and perfect harmony of primeval Nature, but as another, if devastating, facet of Nature. Nature may be Acis and Galatea's perfection of physical form and the pure intensity of their passion, but Nature is also the horror of Polyphemus' being. All this is not meant to suggest that Polyphemus is a prefigurement of Frankenstein's monster, the Romantic, persecuted *Aussenseiter*, who deserves compassion more than annihilation. Robert Jammes' comments on the "humanization" of the cyclops, particularly in his song to Galatea, which, one must recall, does constitute one-fourth of the composition, imply the necessity to shift critical emphasis away from the Beauty and the Beast antithesis, which Dámaso Alonso has defended so insistently, toward underlining the essential human qualities of the monster. We have touched briefly on this matter in our introductory comments to this chapter. We suggest that it may not be necessary to see Polyphemus as a misunderstood, deformed human being in order to accept the consistency between his song and his role as a negative side of Nature; Dámaso Alonso can only find that some parts of the song, at least, are out of place in tone.[17] While a full discussion of the song and its role in the overall structure of the poem must await our presentation of the third movement, suffice it here to repeat our earlier suggestion that Polyphemus may indeed be a human projection of Nature, that we may accept, with Jammes, a certain clear basis of manly humanity in his character. But we must also subscribe to the notion that his is the darker side of humanity or human nature, that side of us which is unspeakable and destructive. That Góngora may be able to perceive the interplay of tender human emotion (in the song to Galatea) and destructive evil, even though spontaneous and unconscious, in one person, bespeaks the increased depth of psychological perception to be found in seventeenth-century literature, as witnessed in the theater of Shakespeare and the fiction of Cervantes. Of course, and in line with his traditional source materials, Góngora has the darker, destructive side of Polyphemus' character dominate, a side of human nature which cannot be doubted since it is given material, symbolic representation in his physical appearance.

Turning specifically to the presentation of the monster's person, we find that there is an internal progression from two stanzas devoted to his appearance (7–8), one to his occupation as a shepherd, in which, in his dominance of the beasts of Nature, he is contrasted with the humble toiler of the earth who must tremble before the fierce animals of twilight, "the doubtful light of day" (9), and three stanzas which detail the cyclops' attendant pastoral attributes, such as his shepherd's purse and his pipes of Pan (10–12). The latter detail brings us back to Nature as a whole, and we have already referred to how the music produced by the monster with his exaggerated instrument causes all of Nature to tremble before it. Aside from the relationship of this facet of his character with the question of the poet's music vs. Polyphemus' music, we are reminded, through the closing epiphonema, of his direct integration or participation in the totality of Nature represented by the microcosm of Sicily. Attention should be paid to a number of details of this stanza, which enjoys the emphasis provided by its being the closing stanza of the presentation of Polyphemus, who is, after all, the motivating focus of the entire composition:

Cera y cáñamo unió (que no debiera)
cien cañas, cuyo bárbaro rüído,
de más ecos que unió cáñamo y cera
albogues, duramente es repetido.
La selva se confunde, el mar se altera,
rompe Tritón su caracol torcido,
sordo huye el bajel a vela y remo:
¡tal la música es de Polifemo! (s. 12)

(Wax and hemp joined, as they should not, a hundred reeds, whose barbarous noise is harshly repeated in more echoes than the pipes that hemp and wax joined. The forest is perplexed, the sea is troubled, Triton breaks his twisted shell, deaf flies the ship by sail and oar; such is the music of Polyphemus[!].)

In passing one should note, since this is the first stanza quoted in full, that one recurring structural feature of Góngora's strophes (which are *octavas reales,* "royal octaves," hendecasyllabic lines rhyming ABABABCC[18]) is the pause between lines 4 and 5. With very few exceptions, all of the strophes of the *Polyphemus* reveal a pause, either full or partial; often the pause marks the division between two distinct halves of the strophe, one concrete and one abstract, or one highly metaphoric and one more or less straightforwardly descriptive. Dámaso Alonso, in his edition of the text from which we are quoting, makes ample references to this internal feature of stanzaic structure.

More directly at issue in this stanza that concludes so emphatically the pivotal characterization of the cyclops is the dominance of negatively charged phrases: "as they should not," "barbarous noise" (which might be taken either as hideous or neutrally rustic),[19] "forest . . . perplexed," "sea . . . troubled," "deaf . . . ship," plus, finally, the force of the exclamatory epiphonema contained in the last line of the stanza. Note here that the binary division of the stanza divides the first four verses that describe the instrument itself from the second four verses which describe its effects upon Nature when played by Polyphemus. The description itself is given an interesting summary unity by the chiasmus "wax and hemp" (line 1)/ "hemp and wax" (line 3), a feature which reinforces how the instrument has been fashioned—although it ought not to have been—from products of Nature, products which are now, by virtue of their conjunction in an instrument that is greater than the sum of its parts (the sense of line 3), turned against Nature and result in its very disruption (the second half of the stanza). Thus by this insistent negative characterization of the musical instrument with which the monster entertains himself, Góngora underscores emphatically at the conclusion of his presentation of his protagonist the extent to which we are to understand how, though a pastoral creature, a shepherd, Polyphemus is essentially at odds with Nature, or at least its typical pastoral evocation.

And too, although the reader is unaware of it at this point, the focusing on the musical instrument as the final, metonymic detail of Polyphemus' character is explainable in terms of the role which that instrument is going to play in stanzas 44–58, first as part of the monster's song to Galatea and then, in the moment of Galatea's passionate attentions to Acis, as a reminder to the nymph of the inescapable presence of her terrible suitor, a foreshadowing, to be sure, of the story's cruel denouement (stanza 44; a specific reference to the pipes and their sound, which startles the entwined couple as they lie upon their bower). Góngora is particularly susceptible to the verbal intensity of metonymy and synecdoche. The latter device can be discovered in virtually every stanza of the poem (e.g., singular nouns, used as concrete mass nouns, rather than the colloquial concrete mass noun: "vine" rather than "vines" or "vineyard"). In the case of the shepherd's pipes, they become a particularly effective metonymy to characterize the cyclops' person here, a detail which is of even greater weight once we understand the integral role played by the song to Galatea which they prelude in the overall representation of Polyphemus' place in the natural scheme of existence.

VI *Galatea: the Nymph-Eve*

The second movement of the composition is the longest and the most complex, covering the thirty stanzas (half the poem), 13–42. Any commentary must be careful, therefore, to avoid a mere description of their complexity and to provide a satisfactory whole of Góngora's poem. Again, in lieu of the 240 lines of text, we indulge in a schematic portrayal:

Galatea	person —	stanza 13–14
	sea lovers —	15–17
	land lovers —	18–22
Acis	transition —	23–24
	person —	25
	discovery of Galatea —	26–27
Galatea's awakening to love	Acis' offerings —	28–32
	discovery of Acis —	33–37
Galatea and Acis' union	transition —	38–39
	union —	40–42

Dámaso Alonso has made much of the juxtaposition of the descriptions of Polyphemus and Galatea, and indeed it would be unfortunate to overlook the effect created by this juxtaposition (cf.

note 6). His comments highlight an antithetical juxtaposition between the hideous (Polyphemus) and the exquisitely beautiful (Galatea), and speaks in terms of a poetic contrast that one might reformulate as the Romantic cliché of the Beauty and the Beast. Of course, Alonso is not interested in seeing in the *Polyphemus* prefigurings of a Romantic *Weltanschauung.* His stress, rather, lies on the poem's concern for a Baroque tension between perfectly harmonious elements of Nature and their disruption by forces which are either evil, chthonic, or monstrous, or all three. Certainly such an assessment is easy at this point in the composition, since the stanzas remain, until the introduction of Acis and the love he awakens in Galatea (ss. 22 ff.), basically descriptive. Thus we are presented first with the detailed description of Polyphemus, his setting, his person, his accoutrements (ss. 4–12) and then with the detailed description of Galatea, her person, her effects on the men who pursue her, and her carefree abandon and concern only with herself (ss. 13–24). Dámaso Alonso has spoken at length of the many contrasts between the two descriptions, and it should not be surprising to find that the poet's rhetoric is organized in terms of suggesting in as effective terms as possible Polyphemus' role as one manifestation of the microcosm that is Sicily and that Galatea is representative of another, whether that opposition be one of Baroque beauty versus Baroque monstrosity, or, as we have suggested, one of the ideal beauty of human aspirations versus those elements of the universal human circumstances which threaten and destroy the former. Polyphemus and Galatea are the two principal focal points of the poem, a fact made evident by the original title, *Fable of Polyphemus and Galatea,* and whatever the two represent in terms of Góngora's Baroque and poetic outlook on the human circumstance, there is no doubt that his juxtaposition of the two from the outset is quite effective. The transition from Polyphemus to Galatea is to be noted; we will later speak of any value such a transition might have as an element of foreshadowing in the subsequent "action" of the poem (note how Galatea, like Polyphemus, is tied to Neptune and the sea):

Ninfa, de Doris hija, la más bella,
adora, que vio el reino de la espuma.
Galatea es su nombre, y dulce en ella
el terno Venus de sus Gracias suma.
Son una y otra luminosa estrella

lucientes ojos de su blanca pluma:
si roca de cristal no es de Neptuno,
pavón de Venus es, cisne de Juno. (s. 13)

(He worships a nymph, the loveliest of Doris' daughters, who saw the kingdom of the foam. Galatea is her name, and gentle Venus leads in her the triad of her graces. The one and the other luminous star are the sparkling eyes of her white plumage: if she is not Neptune's crystal rock, she is Venus' peacock, Juno's swan.)[20]

The structure of the second part of the *Polyphemus,* as can be seen from the foregoing sketch, is almost geometric. Although the presentation of Polyphemus himself occupies only six stanzas (7–12), Galatea is accorded ten, divided into two blocks of five stanzas each on the basis of her introduction and her flight from sea-suitors (ss. 13–17), and also her flight from her land-suitors (ss. 18–22). Each of these two halves of Galatea's presentation ends with an epiphonema, a device which, as Alonso has pointed out in his notes to the text, functions to signal major transitions in the poem; we might call it a form of structural punctuation. We have seen how an epiphonema concludes emphatically the characterization of Polyphemus (s. 12h); the following lines serve to summarize the characterization of Galatea's effect on men, both those creatures of the sea (Glaucus [described in s. 15] and Palaemon [s. 16]) as well as the farmers and shepherds of the land:

. . . ¡Oh cuánto yerra
delfín que sigue en agua corza en tierra! (s. 17g–h)

(O how astray is the dolphin that follows in water the antelope on land!)

¡Revoca, Amor, los silbos, o a su dueño
el silencio del can siga, y el sueño! (s. 22g–h)

(Love, renew the whistlings [of the shepherds], or let the silence of the dog, and sleep, follow its master[!].)

Both of these epiphonema have one thing in common that justifies our quoting them together. Of course, they are a summary of Galatea's effects on her suitors (the second quote, which has presented the commentators with especially difficult problems of interpretation, is to be understood as a synthesis of the abandonment and disarray created among the activities of the island by the young men's mindless pursuit of Galatea). But, in addition to this, one senses a certain tone of reproach toward Galatea. We suggested in the introductory comments to this chapter that one way of understanding Galatea as a pivotal figure of the composition would be in terms of a means of destruction: Galatea as an Eve figure. We are reminded of Góngora's comments on the apple in the second sonnet analyzed in Chapter 3. It is not so much the poet's concern with Christian symbols of the Fall, but with his realization that the concept of the Fall, and the instruments thereof, is a basic human reality which is given one articulation in the symbols and beliefs of Christianity, but which are also recurring motifs in all human experience. Such a realization may have been mostly unconscious and it would be ridiculous even to imply that Góngora and other seventeenth-century intellectuals and artists were concerned with anthropological archetypes *avant la lettre.* Rather we are referring to the implications of Góngora's approach to human nature, an approach which completely bypasses Christian, religious contexts (his religious poetry, generally acknowledged to be inferior, is quite remote from the central concerns of the major works discussed in this study). Thus in the sonnet discussed previously, Góngora can refer to phenomena of human nature and experience that could be formulated in Christian terms of the Fall; the deliberate suppression of explicit religious references can be taken as indicative of his desire to dwell on human nature outside the context of religious myths. Of course the poet uses other myths, those of classical Antiquity, which it is commonplace to assert, at least from our modern point of view, are simply another variant of the same story of the Fall of mankind. Certainly this is one truth which the reader takes away from Ovid's *Metamorphoses* and his stories of the weaknesses and punishments of gods which are only too patently human.

Thus, when we speak of Galatea as an Eve figure, as a temptress, it is not so much in terms of a Christian context. Rather, she possesses a symbolic role in the poem and represents, at least on the most immediate level, ideal human beauty which is completely abandoned to itself (the Spanish word is more precise: Galatea evinces an unconcerned *ensimismamiento*). Toward emphasizing this feature of Galatea's person, the poet dwells at such length on her suitors and on the reckless despair which she evokes in them, as she lightly flees along her garden paths, leaving unconcernedly behind her the wreck of unrequited passion. One of those she spurns is, of course, Polyphemus himself. Although his love for her is mentioned as a form of transition from stanza 12 to 13, from the description of his person to that of Galatea's, it is not referred to again until his song beginning with stanza 43. Nevertheless, Polyphemus is present to a certain degree in the intervening stanzas dealing with Galatea's union with Acis, at least for those readers who know the original story. But quite aside from the problem presented by Galatea and Polyphemus and what she brings of the latter to her relations with Acis (i.e., the cyclops' jealous pursuit of her and his rage when he realizes that another has had what has been denied him), there are many oblique suggestions throughout this second movement of the poem, before the reappearance of Polyphemus and his destructive rage, that Galatea is to be seen as a woman of consummate cruelty and that her person and its incredible beauty represent also a form of destruction or, at best, disruption. Thus the futility of her pursuit by Glaucus and Palaemon summarized by the poet's epiphonemic emphasis in stanza 17 and the disarray in which the island's proud crops and herds are left to fall as farmers and shepherds pursue in vain the nymph, as summarized in the imperative epiphonema of stanza 22.

The ten stanzas given over to the description of Galatea and the disruption created by her suitor's futile pursuit of the unattainable beauty of her body are counterbalanced by ten stanzas assigned to the awakening in her of an intense passion for Acis, a passion which leads ultimately to their union and the jealous destruction of the latter by the enraged and spurned Polyphemus. Five stanzas provide a transition to Galatea's tardy awakening to love (ss. 23–27). In these stanzas, the poet describes Galatea's repose (weary because of her flight from her ardent suitors) beside a fountain, the appearance of Acis and his placement of gifts beside the sleeping Galatea, an altar of unspeakable beauty. It is more important to note that the introduction of Acis is summary. Although he is given something of a description in one stanza (25; where he, also, is presented as of sea origin), Acis' function, it would appear, is only marginal to that of Polyphemus and Galatea. Although destined to receive the brunt of Polyphemus' final mindless rage over what he considers to be Galatea's cruel betrayal of his own attentions, Acis never plays more than an incidental role. It is he who provides the occasion for Galatea's submission to the emotion of love, so ignored previously in her carefree flight from men, and it is he who provides the occasion for the final realization of a "confrontation" between Polyphemus and Galatea and whatever they represent. One might say that Acis is an innocent victim, a victim of Polyphemus' monstrous rage and a victim of Galatea's cruel beauty. However, to the extent that the poem is less concerned with psychological portrayal and more concerned with the depiction of ultimately higher human circumstances, Acis is only of minor importance and, perhaps, one might say, an incidental figure in the staged microcosm of the poem's action. Significantly, the stress is on Galatea's awakening to love and the importance of her subsequent submission to passion, from which she had previously so assiduously fled, in the remaining half of the second part of the composition. Throughout, Acis is only the catalyst, only the circumstance that happens on the scene, for this change in Galatea's person and the reaction which it prompts in Polyphemus.

VII *Galatea and Acis*

The second half of the second part of the poem, which extends from stanza 28 to 42, is divided like the first half into three five-stanza segments, with the first two joined by a common focus. The first ten, thus, deal with Galatea's awakening to love, as she first spies Acis' offerings (which parallel the offerings which other suitors have made to her and which Polyphemus will make to her in his song) and then she discovers Acis, who pretends to sleep as he awaits her reaction; each of these steps requires five stanzas. The poet is primarily concerned, as we have asserted, with depicting the change in Galatea. From the outset a change begins to operate on the nymph: she would flee (as she has fled before from such offerings) but something as yet undefined stays her flight; from a stylistic point of view, the conditional sentence is pivotal in signalling a change in Galatea:

> *La ninfa, pues, la sonorosa plata*
> *bullir sintió del arroyuelo apenas,*
> *cuando, a los verdes márgenes ingrata,*
> *segur se hizo de sus azucenas.*
> *Huyera; mas tan frío se desata*
> *un temor perezoso por sus venas,*

que a la precisa fuga, al presto vuelo,
grillos de nieve fue, plumas de hielo. (s.28)

(The nymph, then, faintly heard the sonorous silver of the rivulet effervesce, when, ungrateful to the green banks, she became a hatchet to their lilies. She would flee, but a lazy fear goes coursing through her veins so coldly that it was to immediate flight, to swift escape, manacles of snow, feathers of ice.)

One should observe how the poet at this point, with Galatea on the brink of her unsuspecting succumbence to passion, reinforces the notion of her cruelty, first through her "ingratitude" in depriving the meadow of the lilies of her limbs and second through the implication, by the use of the contrary-to-fact statement, that her normal response to masculine attentions would be to flee (ungratefully). Line 7 lays particular stress on flight as the metonymy of Galatea's person with the reiteration of "immediate flight, . . . swift escape."

The poet has as one of his unifying motifs throughout the composition (much like Polyphemus' music) that of the offerings of the suitors at the altar of Galatea's beauty. Earlier, in stanzas 18–20, reference is made to the abundant wealth of Sicily and to offerings of that wealth which are left for Galatea, who is described as a "deity" by virtue of either religion or love (s. 19e–h). Now Galatea discovers the offerings left by Acis (s. 29) and is perplexed as to their origin; her confusion and lack of flight set the stage for her domination by love. Stanza 30, taken as a whole, is an example of an implied "Not A, but B" formula, one of Góngora's most cherished rhetorical devices.[21] The first half of the stanza concerns how the gifts are *not* from the usual suitors, the monster and the men of the island. The second half of the stanza, by referring to Cupid and his decision to wound Galatea with his darts, is a displacement for Acis, the worshipper who has left these gifts which so startle the nymph and who will be the one to awaken in her the until then unknown emotion:

No al Cíclope atribuye, no, la ofrenda;
no a sátiro lascivo, ni a otro feo
morador de las selvas, cuya rienda
el sueño aflija, que aflojó el deseo.
El niño dios, entonces, de la venda,
ostentación gloriosa, alto trofeo

quiere que al árbol de su madre sea
el desdén hasta allí de Galatea. (s. 30)

(Not to the Cyclops does she attribute the offering, no; not to the lascivious Satyr, not to any other ugly denizen of the woods, whose reins, which desire weakened, may sleep afflict. The blindfolded boy-god thereupon desires the present disdain of Galatea to be a glorious ostentation, a lofty trophy for his mother's tree.)

Once again, Galatea's haughty disdain for passion is alluded to.

But what is most interesting is the poet's conceitful displacement of Acis by Cupid and the whole range of allusions evoked by his introduction, a circumstance that reinforces our claim that Acis is really quite marginal to the action of the narrative. Rather than construct the stanza so that we are told that the nymph realizes that the gifts are *not* from the cyclops nor the lascivious satyr, but from Acis, who is to inspire her with passion, the poet states that, once the negative is accepted, Cupid, through first the gifts and then Acis' person (ss. 33–37), will wound Galatea. To say that Cupid is moved to action is a conceitful way of saying that an emotional transformation takes place in the woman as the result of a realization, perhaps as yet unconscious, that the gifts are from one whom she can respond to (the positive segment of the formula). Stanza 31 describes the beginning of Cupid's labors, and the reader should not be surprised to see that Galatea, as those labors begin to take their effect, is described as *El monstro [sic] de rigor, la fiera brava . . .* (The monster of severity, the wild beast . . . [s. 31e])." This hunt metaphor not only once again reminds us of Galatea's cruelty, but also reinforces how Cupid's conquest is effected through an arrow wound: Galatea's breast, in a startling image, is described as becoming the crystal quiver for Cupid's arrow (s. 31c–d). As a whole, the sequence of ten stanzas that detail Galatea's awakening to passion deserve close attention for the poet's skill in the use of conceit in describing through minute transformations the overall change in Galatea's emotions. We are reminded here, although there is the tendency to forget it when we talk about the "action" and the "meaning" of the denouement, that Góngora's Baroque interest lies primarily in the use of language to evoke statically a revealing circumstance rather than to produce a narrative per se. Of course, the *Polyphemus* does involve a distinct "event" and the poet's choice of subject matter does tie him to evoking the general outlines of that event. But there are segments of the poem that reveal what a later period will call *tempo lento* and what might best be described with the contemporaneous term *ecphrasis* or *amplificatio,* segments where the poet dwells in elaborate detail on the evocation of a circumstance.[22] Such are the ten stanzas devoted to Galatea's change of heart, and the critic cannot help but observe that such a procedure is most assuredly to become the entire principle of the *Solitudes,* which date from roughly the same time as the *Polyphemus.*

One would expect that the series of stanzas on Galatea's awakening to passion would conclude with an epiphonema. Instead, the poet is content to summarize the effect of Cupid's magic:

> *que en sus paladïones Amor ciego,*
> *sin romper muros, introduce fuego.* (s. 37g–h)

(for into her Palladia blind Love, without breaking through walls, introduces fire.)

The remaining block of five stanzas that close the second movement or part of the poem concern the consummation of the intense passion that has been awakened between these two children of Nature. Acis shows himself to be appropriately aggressive: he has now assumed the role of Love personified, his offerings and the vision of his perfect human form have worked their effect upon Galatea, and he undertakes now to make his what has been so maddeningly denied the nymph's previous suitors. These stanzas contain some of the most intensely erotic lines of seventeenth-century poetry (as opposed to some of the entertaining but less intense scatological poetry of the same period). Smith has observed apropos of these stanzas that: "The love-making of Acis and Galathea [*sic*] (stanzas 41, 42) has no emotional content, and it is even performed without a word being spoken. There is a fine biological beauty about it, a sort of animal simplicity and a Lawrentian purity. Lorca saw this with wonderful clarity when he observed that the eroticism is one of floral sexuality, a sexuality of stamen and pistle" (p. 222).

Smith's point, of course well taken, is that Acis and Galatea are integral parts of their natural setting, of what we have called the Sicilian microcosm. We might add in line with our interest in the structural characteristics of the poem, in how the poet organizes his material for greatest rhetorical effect, that it is necessary and effective to close this segment of the poem with a stressing of Acis' and Galatea's integration with their natural surroundings (recall that they retire to make love in a secret bower, attended by softly cooing doves). To stress such an integration is one way of emphasizing, when we move on to contemplate the monster in his song and then in his rage, how both the lovers and the cyclops represent contending forces of Nature, perfect harmony on the one hand and inevitable destruction on the other. In the last analysis, the abnormal destructive forces of Nature may not be finally triumphant (this is why we can call them "abnormal" as opposed to a Schopenhaurian conception of them as the norm)—the poem concludes on a note of another integration with Nature: Acis' return to the sea as a crystalline stream. But at this point in the composition it is necessary that the poet structure his narrative in order to best highlight Polyphemus' revenge. We are to see the latter as an "interference," so to speak, of what has been presented, cameo fashion, as almost an emblematic representation of perfect natural harmony:

No a las palomas concedió Cupido
juntar de sus dos picos los rubíes,
cuando al clavel el joven atrevido
las dos hojas le chupa carmesíes.
Cuantas produce Pafo, engendra Gnido,
negras vïolas, blancos alhelíes,
llueven sobre el que Amor quiere que sea
tálamo de Acis ya y de Galatea. (s. 42)

(Hardly had Cupid allowed the doves to join the rubies of their two bills, when the emboldened youth sucks the two crimson leaves of the carnation. May all the black violets, white gillyflowers that Pahpos produces, Cnidos engenders, rain down upon what Love desires to be the bridal couch of Acis and of Galatea.)

VIII *Artifice Triumphant*

Stanza 42 closes with a direct reference to the two lovers by name, a way of summarizing the passionate union which has obtained between them. The twenty-one stanzas of the poem deal with the implications and the consequences of that union. It is here where Góngora departs most noticeably from his source in Ovid; an attempt to understand the nature of that departure and its rationale are unquestionably necessary to grasp fully what the overall meaning of Góngora's Polyphemus is. The structure of these final stanzas does not require any schematic representation for their understanding. Only two segments are involved: the reintroduction of Polyphemus and his appeal in song to Galatea to accept his attentions (ss. 43–58) and his discovery, by accident, of the lovers, locked in their bliss but disturbed by the monster's dissonant song (dissonant by definition because Polyphemus is a monster and dissonant because it disrupts their idyll and the perfection of their passionate integration with Nature), his ensuing rage and destruction of Acis, and the latter's return to the sea (ss. 59–63).

There are three significant aspects of Góngora's departure from Ovid. In the first place, Góngora places Polyphemus' long song to Galatea at the end of the poem, devoting at least one-fourth of the entire composition to this amorous appeal to the sea nymph. Part of those sixteen stanzas (actually fifteen if we discount stanza 43, which reintroduces the cyclops) involves a four-stanza *exemplum*, the monster's story of his rescue of a shipwrecked merchant. Out of gratitude for Polyphemus' Samaritan attentions, the merchant gives him his wealthy cargo, and Polyphemus is now offering it all to Galatea as tokens of his passionate ardor toward her.

This *exemplum*, aside from its presence as an addition of the poet to his source material, is interesting for the more important detail of the portrait which it provides of the cyclops at this point. Polyphemus describes himself as considerably changed in nature, and the *exemplum* is his proof of that change (ss. 54–58). Where before he had hung in his cave as trophies of his dominion over Sicily the heads of lost travelers, his cave now serves as a hostel to the wandering pilgrim (stanza 54 in particular). Finally, Góngora has Polyphemus indulge himself in his song as an act of spontaneous emotional outpouring, unaware that Galatea hears his song as she lies in the arms of Acis (in Ovid, the cyclops sings out of despair or frustration over his knowledge that the nymph has already given herself to another after denying him). Also, as we have already pointed out, Ovid's poem ends with a somewhat more detailed description of Acis' metamorphosis (after all, the entire point of departure of Ovid's tales), suggesting a direct preoccupation with the triumph of the monster's power. Góngora devotes barely two stanzas to the material transformation of Galatea's lover, who as he is crushed turns into a crystalline stream that returns to the sea. The poet implies unquestionably that the change itself and the reintegration with the sea, the completion of the life cycle, to be received by Galatea's mother, Doris, with pious lamentations (ss. 62–63), are to be seen as a form of triumph not of Polyphemus' monstrousness, but of the transcendent passion of the two lovers.

The foregoing are the major characteristics of the concluding segment of Góngora's poem and represent some significant ways in which he departs from Ovid's version of the story, a version which most of the other Renaissance poets retold verbatim. Identification of these characteristics, however, is not enough. In order truly to understand Góngora's attitude toward his material—to understand the "rhetoric" of that material, to use a more voguish term—it is necessary to suggest a function for these characteristics. The critic is confronted here with an almost insoluble paradox of literary interpretation. From one point of view, and certainly that of Góngora and his highly learned audience, these departures from the source play a distinctly emphatic role. To the extent that they go counter to the reader's expectations on the basis of his acquaintance with Ovid, the poet is calling special attention to what the poet does that does *not* follow the model, and a great deal can be said at this point concerning Góngora's probable and significant reasons for modifying his material. The modern reader, however, cannot be expected to have the same acquaintance with the classics, and traditional teachers of literature cry in vain that they should. Thus this segment of the poem, while it may not be read in a complete vacuum, does not have the significance for the departures that it does for the aforementioned and earlier audience; even where he has the critic's textual notes, the modern reader, in any case, does not find it unusual for source material to be modified completely, and imitation has become a hazy principle of composition.

On the other hand, the modern critic does well to insist that if those segments of the composition which were significant for an earlier reader because of their departure from the model are indeed central to an understanding of the poem, a consideration of them within the totality of the composition will, nevertheless, provide the same basis of emphasis. (Dividing the poem into segments that follow the model routinely and those that depart from it significantly is, of course, not a critical approach seriously based on organic unity.) Thus, a reading that does not compare the poem with Ovid's *Metamorphoses* should identify anyway, precisely because Góngora is a brilliant poet who does more than slavishly retell a hackneyed story, the outstanding characteristics of the last segment of the poem. For example, given the opening presentation of Polyphemus, one should be surprised to hear his song and to perceive the change that has taken place in his person. That is to say, the reader should be alerted to the possible significance of the reintroduction of the cyclops, after a lapse of thirty stanzas (half of the poem), in an entirely different light than when we left him back in stanza 12. Moreover, the concluding portrait of Polyphemus in this stanza (he is mentioned only in passing in the next stanza as loving Galatea, who then occupies the full attention of the narrative) is contained in the epiphonema that speaks of his thunderous and discordant music. Now, in stanza 44, he reappears, with the same pipes, but in order to sing a song of love to Galatea in which he speaks of his (to the reader and to threatened Sicily) wondrous transformation. Furthermore the monster's reappearance is tied in, quite artfully and ingeniously, with the final heights of passion of the two secret lovers. Recall that the monster entones his appeal to Galatea unaware of her involvement with Acis:

Arbitro de montañas y ribera,
aliento dio, en la cumbre de la roca,
a los albogues que agregó la cera,
el prodigioso fuelle de su boca;
la ninfa los oyó, y ser más quisiera
breve flor, hierba humilde, tierra poca,
que de su nuevo tronco vid lasciva,
muerta de amor, y de temor no viva.
Mas—cristalinos pámpanos sus brazos—
amor la implica, si el temor la anuda,
al infelice olmo que pedazos
la segur de los celos hará aguda.
Las cavernas en tanto, los ribazos
que ha prevenido la zampoña ruda,
el trueno de la voz fulminó luego:
¡referidlo, Pïerides, os ruego! (ss. 44–45)

(Arbiter of mountains and shore, on the summit of the cliff the prodigious bellows of his mouth gave breath to the reeds that the wax joined; the

nymph heard them and would rather be a small flower, humble plant, and little earth, than the sportive vine of his new trunk, dead she was of love and lifeless with fear.[23]
But (her arms crystal vineshoots) love binds her, while fear ties her to the unhappy elm which the sharp ax of jealousy will cut to pieces. Meanwhile the thunder of the voice then struck the caves, the hills which the rude pipes had forewarned: set it forth, Pierides, I beg you.)

What it appears to us that Góngora is attempting to do (and for this reason we have quoted the two stanzas fully) is to set up a context of foreshadowing and violent denouement (figuratively and literally). The two lovers have retired to consummate their passion, attended by the metonymic cooing of doves, the erotic music of a profound physical love. Immediately thereupon their idyll is interrupted, shattered, by the sound of Polyphemus' *zampoña ruda,* a phrase that means both "rude" (in the sense of unpleasant) as well as "rustic" pipes. Stanza 45 goes beyond the foreshadowing of tragedy suggested by Galatea's fear, as intense at the sound of the music as her just concluded passion, to refer quite explicitly, if metaphorically, to the destruction through jealousy of the trunk to which she, the lascivious vine of the preceding stanza, is adhered (s. 45c–d).

But the violent juxtaposition of the lovers' idyll with the prompt reappearance of the monster, the function of his music as a symbol of his imposition upon tranquil Nature, and the unmistakably central epiphonema which concludes his reintroduction (s. 45h), all contribute to making the reader aware that he has reached a point of narrative synthesis, of a climactic coming together of the major elements and conflicts of the narrative. It is vital to note how the poet phrases his epiphonema in terms of the venerable rhetorical commonplace of expressive incompetence; in order to stress how his material is so weighty or tragic, the poet confesses himself unable to relate it adequately, often appealing to someone acknowledgedly more able than himself, such as the Muses themselves. Góngora does not make notable use in his poetry of hackneyed medieval rhetorical commonplaces, and understandably. But his use here of what in Spanish has been called *no puedo más* (I can't go on) is effective in signaling the momentous nature of what is happening or about to happen.

But the climax does not come immediately, and the poet seems to back away from the intense tone that he has created through the foreshadowing created by juxtaposition of lovers and pursuing monster, by the change in language from the eroticism of the conjugal bower to the nymph's horror, and by the shift from the music of the doves to Polyphemus' music, already possessing an established symbolic function. Some critics have been surprised by this backing away and have been at a loss to measure adequately the role played by the cyclops' song and, more to the point, by his self-confessed change of character. Even Dámaso Alonso, who, more than any other critic in the century, has contributed so overwhelmingly to our comprehension of Góngora's art, is forced to wonder if the stanzas in question, in particular the *exemplum*, are not out of place. He calls them, frankly, strange (see his commentary on these stanzas in his edition of the poem). Normally Alonso is willing to follow the standard critical procedure of assuming that the poet knows what he is about and of working backwards from what the poet does to an explanation of why he may have done it, in order to arrive at an understanding of how the troublesome passage may contribute after all to the overall unity of the work. On many occasions, Alonso has proceeded in this fashion and has proposed a reading which is "correct" because it "fits" the work as a whole (see, for example, his comments on stanza 11, a stanza which is not central to the poem but which has shown itself to be the most difficult one of the entire poem to understand[24]). What, then, are we to say about the development of the *Polyphemus* at this point, which moves from the final passion of the two lovers (up to stanza 42), the reappearance of the monster (stanza 43), his disruption with his pipes of the lovers' idyll, the nymph's horror, and the reference to an imminent jealous rage (ss. 44–45), the cyclops' song in which he relates, as proof of his love for Galatea, his change of character and his good-Samaritan attentions to a shipwrecked merchant (ss. 55–58)?

What is involved here is more than just the "humanization" of the monster, which Robert Jammes has focused on in order to reject the standard emphasis on Polyphemus as the monstrous side of Nature. We repeat once again that modern Romantic and/or psychological motives are not easily attributable to Góngora, whose poetry is, after all, scarcely narrative-oriented anyway. We suggest, rather, that Góngora has simply taken advantage again of the emphatic value of a well-placed juxtaposition. We have seen how, in the early part of the poem, the two facets of Nature represented by Polyphemus and Galatea are juxtaposed by the movement from stanza 12, which concludes the detailing of the cyclops' monstrosity with the epiphonema on his music, to stanza 13, which introduces Galatea, the nymph in whom "Venus synthesizes sweetly the charms of her three Graces." In the final segments of the poem what Góngora has done is to shift Polyphemus' personality perceptively in order to underline his "willingness," so to speak, to make himself more worthy of the attentions of that perfect image of Venus. Furthermore, the momentary softening of Polyphemus' monstrousness, the surprising "humanization" of his character which so eloquently bespeaks the effect upon him, as upon other suitors, of Galatea's femininity, are but a prelude to the horrible and uncontrolled fury which he will release, now returned fully to his "normal," enduring personality, upon the unlucky Acis. What we are saying, then, is that Góngora's "stepping back" from the tension which he creates in stanzas 44–45 is a form of dramatic emphasis for the cyclops' jealous rage when he discovers the degree to which he has been spurned. Indeed, his song justifies his rage to the extent that we see how his conscious "humanization" has been utterly in vain all along. Galatea is not his, will never be his, and has already been, to the fullest depths of physical love, another's.

A few pages back we used the word "transformation" to refer to Polyphemus' apparent change of character that so bewilders Alonso and misleads (we feel) Jammes. The word was purposely chosen in order to underline how that change is itself a form of foreshadowing: Góngora's procedure is deliberately and appropriately rhetorical at this point. He is aware of how Polyphemus' rage can gain in intensity by having it the result, not of simply an extension of his customarily monstrous self, as projected by the opening stanzas of the poem, but of a sudden return to that monstrousness as the result of the "betrayal" of his willingness to indulge, through his "humanization," the woman whom he would now have won, not by pursuit, but by a sympathetic approach. Thus, his self-portrait (ss. 49–53) and his offering at the altar of her beauty the gifts which he had received from the shipwrecked merchant (ss. 57–58) parallel the earlier portrait of Acis and his gifts which so effectively conquered Galatea's heart. Of course, Polyphemus is to have no such luck and it is precisely his realization that all he has done he has done in vain that unleashes once again, overcoming his transitory tenderness toward Galatea, his mythic, cyclopean fury. The object of that fury is Acis, thus fulfilling the implied parallel between the two, with Galatea as the focal point, the prize to be won. Acis is, in a sense that we have already alluded to, a victim of the antithetical relationship between Polyphemus and Galatea, and it is upon his body that vengeance of the evil side of Nature is unleashed. But it is also his body which enjoys the deification by the perfect forces of Nature, as the permanent transformation (as opposed to Polyphemus' fleeting transformation out of futile amorous sentiment) is affected by Galatea, her mother, Doris, and the other water deities. As he is crushed by the cyclops' missile, he is changed into a water god that returns to the sea, to the origin and the symbol of an integrated Nature. It is upon this note that the composition ends. Góngora concludes, not with a reference to the triumph of the forces of evil or of Nature deformed, but with the image of the divinized Acis' final union with transcendent Nature:

Sus miembros lastimosamente opresos
del escollo fatal fueron apenas,
que los pies de los árboles más gruesos
calzó el líquido aljófar de sus venas.
Corriente plata al fin sus blancos huesos,
lamiendo flores y argentando arenas,
a Doris llega, que, con llanto pío,
yerno lo saludó, lo aclamó río. (s. 63)

(Hardly had his limbs been lamentably crushed by the deadly rock than the liquid pearl of his veins covered the feet of the stoutest trees. Finally, his white bones running argent, licking flowers and silvering sands, he reaches Doris, who with merciful lament greeted him as a son-in-law, acclaimed him as a river.)

With this stanza, we have returned to the language and to the tone of the passionate union between Acis and Galatea in stanza 42, a union now made permanent despite, but also as the direct result of, the intervention of the forces of unpleasant Nature represented by Polyphemus.

It is true on one immediate level that Góngora's poem deals not with the perfection of Nature implied by an earlier Renaissance pastoral literature, but with tensions and antithetical forces of Nature which figures of human beings are caught up in. Nevertheless, a close reading of Góngora's organization of his material demonstrates that, despite the traditional emphasis on the cyclops, as manifested in the poem's passing as simply the *Polyphemus* rather than the *Fable of Polyphemus and Galatea*, Góngora was interested in showing a form of triumph over the disruptive forces of Nature. The latter exist and are inescapable, as Galatea and Acis must finally learn. But unlike the overall cynical sense of the story of Angélica and Medoro, whose idyll we are given emphatically to understand will be tragically and irrevocably destroyed by the omnipotent Count Roland, the true symbol of the inevitable destruction of what is humanly of value, we take away from the *Polyphemus* the quite different sense that the ideal can triumph ultimately, that out of monstrous destruction a deification of the ideal can be realized. To be sure, Góngora does not imply a stoic ethos in his poem. After all, we must remember that, unlike the all-too-human Angélica, Medoro, and the Count, the figures of the long narrative poem are not human beings, but symbols of Nature with superhuman origins and powers. They are abstract figures both because they must be interpreted in terms of the smaller human scale and because they never fulfill any role other than that of eponyms of well-defined forces of Nature. To this extent, Góngora may well be speaking in terms of the triumph of art, of the artifice created deliberately. After all, Acis' metamorphosis and deification is the deliberate act of the water divinities through the intercession of Galatea and her mother, and not just simply the automatic consequence of the superiority of the beauty to the monstrous. We mentioned earlier how there is a certain parallelism implied by the poem between the poet's creative act and the creative—as well as destructive—acts of Nature, between his (assumedly perfect) song and the monster's unmistakably hideous song. Poetry, though it must deal with the inevitable forces of evil and discord in Nature (the Christian's sense of omnipresent original sin), is the ultimate triumph of perfection, the permanent imposition of an ideal, objective artifice.

It is perhaps in these abstract terms that Góngora's emphasis on beauty in the poem, which involves both the preponderance of attention accorded the encounter between the two lovers (some thirty stanzas) and the emphasis given the triumph of what Galatea represents symbolically over what Polyphemus represents, must be understood. The imposition of material perfection—the metamorphosis of Acis, the poem itself, as well as the poem promised by the poet in stanza 3 on his patron, naturally the paragon of courtly perfection—is the consequence of a conscious effort. Certainly, for those critics who believe as we do that the *Polyphemus* is Góngora's most perfect example of poetic art, there can be little doubt that the abstract ideal attained material form in this one work.

CHAPTER 5

Las Soledades

I *General Characterization*

THE *Soledades (Solitudes)* represent not only a culmination of Góngora's poetic production, but also a celebration of awareness in Baroque extravagance. Góngora sensed all the energy of the Renaissance liberation of the arts and sciences from theology, and his response here (and in contrast to the *Polyphemus*) is a highly complex and innovative encomium to the harmonious and beautiful world of Nature, a Nature which indeed is utopian in every sense of the word. By combining religious and sensuous overtones, Góngora draws the reader into a pastoral Arcadia which throbs with fertility, colors, abundance, virtue, peace, and vital physical and spiritual relationships. It is a world that bespeaks a vision of man's place in the natural order and man's relationship to man. The poem of some two thousand lines (1091 in the first *Solitude;* 979 in the second) reflects the Horatian manner in its topical praise of the ideal and rustic life of the country and its condemnation of the futile and empty life of the court.

Góngora, who had himself returned to live a bucolic existence in the country to write the *Solitudes*, published the two parts of his poem in 1613 and 1614. Literary critics of the seventeenth century insisted that he planned to write four parts; but he wrote only two, and the second is apparently incomplete. Pellicer, writing in 1630, supported the idea that the four "solitudes" were to represent the four ages of man, while Díaz de Rivas believed that Góngora intended to write on the solitudes of the fields, the seashore, the woods, and the desert.[1] But we really lack any useful evidence as to what Góngora envisioned in the way of an overall structure for the *Solitudes*. Robert Jammes argues in his recent study that it was only casual conjecture that Góngora meant to write more than two solitudes. Jammes believes that Góngora meant to write only one poem with the plural title, *Soledades*. Jammes feels moreover that when Góngora finished the composition, he had as usual bits and pieces left over, so he wrote a second *Soledad*.[2] (A rather reasonable theory since Góngora left numerous unfinished works: a panegyric, an unfinished play, etc.) For his work Góngora chose the irregular *silva* (literally, "forest," and, by extension, "miscellany"—seven- and eleven-syllable lines with no fixed order of strophic length or rhyme); it is a meter which permits an extreme flexibility of composition.

The *Solitudes* represent unquestionably Góngora's most ambitious poem and perhaps the most difficult and most mature of his artistic creations: he leads the reader through a labyrinth of intellectual complexities by means of his metaphors, conceits, and erudite allusions. But in spite of digressions and descriptions, the plot of the poem is extremely simple:[3]

The First *Solitude* (by lines)

[1–37: The dedication to the Duque de Béjar.]

1–21: It is spring and an unnamed shipwrecked youth is cast ashore; he is a "pilgrim of love," rejected by a *belle dame sans merci* of the court and estranged from the city.

22–89: The youth wanders about, scales some cliffs, and is guided to the light of a cottage.

90–175: He is kindly received by some goatherds with whom he spends the night in pastoral comfort.

176–221: Upon awaking at dawn, the youth accompanies one of the goatherds to a rocky promontory from where he can survey the majestic scenery of the countryside.

222–36: Some hunters who are pursuing a wolf pass by; the goatherds joins them.

237–80: The youth delights in the music and dance of some beautiful mountain maidens who have gathered to attend a wedding.

281–334: A group of mountain boys arrive on the scene, bearing gifts of beasts and birds for the marriage feast.

335–59: The weary boys stop to rest and to sleep by a stream. They courteously greet the young stranger.

360–506: An old shepherd who has lost a son at sea recounts the dangers of nautical explorations (a subtle denunciation of Spanish seafaring, commercialism, and cupidity).

507–13: The procession to the wedding continues.

514–30: The old shepherd invites the wandering youth to the wedding.

531–72: The youth accepts and enjoys the walk through the Arcadian forest. He listens to the songs of the girls and the boasts of the shepherds concerning their forthcoming victories in the sports contests.

573–615: They stop to rest by a stream in the midst of all Nature's splendor: "Spring is shod in April's green and clad in May's magnificence."

616–29: Other maidens, relatives of the bridegroom, join the party.

630–41: Night falls as the party hurries to reach the village.

642–58: They reach the village, which is aglow with light: the rays of sunset illuminate the spire of the church while a host of torches blaze at Hymen's shrine.

659–704: The old shepherd leads the youth to a poplar grove, where the latter is intoxicated by the magnificence of the revelry, dancing, and singing. Night and fatigue finally overcome the party.

705–31: It is the next day and the youth meets the bride and groom.

732–66: Upon witnessing the happiness of the young lovers in rustic simplicity, the youth becomes sad and recalls his own ill fortune. His dark thoughts are diverted by the marriage hymn sung by a chorus of beautiful maidens and handsome young men.

767–844: Hymen is invoked in song to bless the couple with prosperity and children.

845–51: Everyone goes to the church and then on to the humble straw dwelling of the bride's father.

852–82: The country hospitality, the joyous guests, and the abundant wedding banquet impress the youth.

883–92: Twelve maidens dance.

893–943: A nymph sings a song wishing the newlyweds a long and felicitous life filled with good fortune and moderate prosperity.

944–1064: Everyone attends the athletic contests: wrestling, jumping and running, the classical games of competitive sports.

1065–91: It is nightfall and the festive party accompanies the bride and groom to their abode, where Venus, "who knows that feathers are Love's most fitting battleground," has prepared their wedding bed.

The Second *Solitude* (by lines)

1–32: At dawn the next day, the pilgrim finds himself by the river with a group of country folk.

33–41: Two fishermen pass by in a boat; one is singing a song.
42–59: A second vessel appears to take away some of the wedding guests.
60–112: The youth joins the two fishermen who have great success in casting their nets and catching all sorts of fish.
113–71: The protagonist sings of his melancholy and ill-fated love. When he dies, he wants to be buried in the sea, where (as also on land) he has lived in exile and alienation. He has been wandering for five years because of his bold love.
172–207: The two fishermen and the protagonist reach the fishermen's hut on a tiny isle.
208–43: The fishermen's father greets them, and his six pretty daughters graciously welcome the youth.
244–313: The old father shows his guest the natural glories of the island, which include swans, doves, rabbits, bees, and goats.
314–60: The daughters serve dinner in a nook of poplar trees; all sit silently, enjoying the music of the water and the harmonious tones of the birds. As they eat, Neptune also dines under the sea with the sirens. (A brilliant juxtaposition in its integration of man with the mythical force of Nature, the fisherman's humble "court" with Neptune's legendary one.)
361–87: A simple prayer of thanks is said by the father after the meal. Then the pilgrim implores the old man to be content with his peaceful life and to abandon fishing.
388–511: In a piscatory eclogue the old man relates how he no longer goes to sea but allows his children to fish. He recounts the prowess of his chaste and lovely daughters: Filódoces bravely killed a savage seal with a spear and Efire all alone speared a monstrous fish which she let escape. Later she conquers a massive sturgeon.
512–41: It is night and the sorrowful song of two young fishermen is to be heard. They are Lycidas and Micón, who are in love with Leucipe and Cloris, daughters of the old fisherman.
542–611: By turns Lycidas and Micón sing of their love for the girls since childhood and of their hopes to marry. They fear that their love will kill them and that their boats will serve as their tombs.
612–44: Night itself, Cupid, the two beloved girls, as well as the others are all deeply stirred by their song. The youth, who has himself experienced the anguish of love, begs the old man to accede to the lovers' request.

645–51: The father gives his consent and so Cupid, sailing on a silver half-shell (his arrows as oars), leads the love-struck fishermen to their future father-in-law.

652–76: The poet, in an aside, addresses himself to the capriciousness of Love, who favors humble lads and who has been a cruel rebel to the pilgrim/youth.

677–90: At dawn the protagonist departs in a boat with his two fishing companions.

691–712: From their vessel they admire the beauty of a castle and hear sounds of a trumpet.

713–830: A description of the hunt creates a fascinating visual feast. The hunters rush out on their purebred horses with all sorts of hunting birds (a falcon, a saker, a gerfalcon, a sparrowhawk, a lanner, a hawk, a British goshawk and an owl). These are followed by a dog and then by a noble prince; the group rushes to the sandbanks of a lagoon.

831–48: A flycatcher quickly leads the flight of frightened birds meant to be the prey of the hunting birds.

849–57: The sparrowhawk pursues the flycatcher.

858–64: The youth, as the perennial witness of all the happenings in the poem, observes the flight of the sparrowhawk and several details of the perfect landscape.

865–74: The frightened flycatcher, seeking refuge in some reeds, is driven out by the hunters and killed by the sparrowhawk.

875–914: A flock of flying ravens block the sun, causing an owl (the accuser, we are told, of Proserpine) to try to fly in the apparent night. The ravens, jealous of the golden eyes of the owl, pounce upon him. Then the ravens are pursued by a gerfalcon from above and a saker from below.

915–36: One raven is trapped and killed by the two hawks.

937–79: The hunters, accompanied by their weary horses and birds, reach some huts whose owners are away fishing or cultivating the land. The poem breaks off or ends at this point.

Immediately one's attention is called to the apparent loose narrative structure of the composition and to its difficult syntax and vocabulary. Góngora uses extensively all the techniques of *culteranismo* and *conceptismo* discussed in Chapter 1 in order to create an impressive and memorable Baroque work in which he departs radically from what had become traditional form. That is, as an example of the reaction against the artificial and vacuous Court, Góngora eulogizes the rustic life of the peasant in his natural setting via his use of a *stylus gravis.* For Góngora, the peasants with their simple lifestyle are the real heroes of life, and thus in his work they are shown to live nobly and to speak eruditely. This vision as well as its attendant poetic technique was audacious in that Góngora turned away from the classical standard norm of poetry whereby only noble subjects and themes were treated with the sublime language of the *stylus gravis.* Instead, his humble characters appear as they are (and they are not simply noblemen dressed as shepherds as in much of Renaissance pastoral literature); yet they speak and are treated with dignity, complexity, and subtlety. Góngora artistically views the peasants as in harmony with nature and the universe; such noble creatures and their pastoral life are indeed the source of beauty, truth, and the meaning of existence. Translated into modern terms, it may be said that Góngora made the *Solitudes* an event, an innovation, and a happening.

II *Literary Problems* of the Solitudes

Ever since the Spanish Renaissance, and especially since the twentieth century, a great many works have been written about the "Cordoban Swan" and thousands upon thousands of words have been written about the *Solitudes.* Chapter 1 has already characterized the heated debates among the literary critics of the Baroque regarding Góngora's poetry, particularly the *Polyphemus* and the *Solitudes.* But it is the Spanish scholar and poet Dámaso Alonso who in this century has done the most to establish Góngora's *Solitudes* as one of the most brilliant and innovative poems of the Western literary tradition. Alonso's criticism has played a major part in the revival and reevaluation of Góngora. Alonso's perceptive textual and linguistic analyses help to disentangle much of the dense, Gongoristic syntax and language in order to reveal the artistic genius of the poet. The year 1927 marked the three-hundredth anniversary of Góngora's birth, and in that year Alonso made a valuable contribution with his first edition of the *Solitudes.* His edition not only contains copious notes, but also provides a prose translation to facilitate comprehension of the work. Although the

Solitudes is difficult in the "aristocratic" tradition of Spanish writing, Alonso argues for the poem as a uniquely meaningful work filled with the deliberately contrived artistry of the late Renaissance.

Another major work of criticism by Alonso, *La lengua poética de Góngora (The Poetic Language of Góngora),* published in 1935 but written in 1927, treats problems such as hyberbaton, learned vocabulary, and syntactic constructions in order to clarify meaning in Góngora's works; among other things, Alonso destroys the myth that there were two Góngoras: an early, facile poet as opposed to a late, complicated artist. Indeed, by concentrating his attention on the *Solitudes,* Alonso has helped to unfold the beauty, the comprehensibility, and the unity of Góngora's work and to clearly position Góngora as an artist who intensified and synthesized the major trends of Spanish Renaissance poetry. And Alonso not only concerns himself with the meaning of the *Solitudes,* but with what the poem does. That is, the poet transcends mere syntactic structures and produces a hermetic world of sound and meaning.

Most significant is the fact that Góngora continues to provide the reader with an aesthetic adventure in the intellectual as well as the sensorial sense. Throughout his scholarly career Alonso has continued to refine his work on Góngora from the points of view of poetic technique, biography, and textual criticism. In 1961, in *Cuatro poetas españoles (Four Spanish Poets),* Alonso addressed himself to the significance of Góngora between 1927 and 1961. In the essay "Góngora entre sus dos centenarios (1927–1961)" ("Góngora Between the Centenary of his Birth and the Centenary of his Death"), Alonso, a bit less enthusiastic but supporting Góngora as an outstanding creator of great and formal poetry, confessed that there was an absence of commitment to human themes and concerns in his poetry.[4]

Perhaps Góngora himself was his own best critic, given the fact that he was quite aware of his own complexity and obscurity. That is, he appreciated his preference for an "aristocratic" approach to literature. (Alonso would have this aristocratic approach as a constant in Spanish literary tradition and not just in Góngora's "aberrant" works.) In a letter which Góngora wrote in defense of the *Solitudes,* he justifies the artistic merit of Ovid's poetic obscurity on the grounds that his poetry not only "educates," but also can serve to *avivar el ingenio* (awaken the mind).[5] Góngora felt that his *Solitudes* can rest on the same justification: "This is precisely what Your Honor will find in my *Solitudes* if you are able to go beyond the surface and discover the mysterious quality which they conceal."[6] In the same letter Góngora mentioned that his *Solitudes,* with all the images, complex tropes and allusions, could lead the reader to the source of truth. Apparently, according to Góngora, the *Solitudes* contain some philosophical content as well as technical difficulties and obscure erudition. Moreover, in the same letter he referred to the aesthetics of his poem, thereby demonstrating a concern for the value of his poetry in linguistic terms: "Because I am honorable, in two ways do I consider that this poetry has been honorable to more: if it is understood by the learned, it will provide me with authority, it being a necessary circumstance to esteem that our language, because of my work, has managed to reach the perfection and sublimity of Latin . . ."[7]

The Generation of 1927 in Spain found a great deal of inspiration and beauty in Góngora's difficulty and formalism. Famous poets like Pedro Salinas, García Lorca, and Jorge Guillén, not to mention Dámaso Alonso, wrote homages and poetry in honor of Góngora in 1927. The facets of Gongorism that enchanted these then young poets were verbal artifice, art for art's sake, technical innovation, and Góngora's form of "pure poetry." García Lorca seems to sum up the appreciation and admiration of his group for Góngora and his genius in a lecture entitled "La imagen poética en Góngora" ("Poetic Imagery in Góngora"): "One must not read Góngora but study him. He loved objective beauty, pure and useless beauty, free of communicable grievings. The originality of don Luis de Góngora, aside from the purely grammatical, is in his method of harvesting images. He composed the great lyrical poem with hitherto-unused proportions: the *Solitudes.* And this great poem sums up all the pastoral lyrical sentiment of all the Spanish poets who preceded him."[8]

In brief, the problems in the *Solitudes* may be viewed as: (a) difficulty of language and structure; (b) a lack of an obvious coherence in the poem; (c) purist poetry, no concern for human, everyday experience; (d) an unfinished work; (e) confusion of genres in the poem; (f) lack of stylistic decorum; (g) allegedly a poem which employs the theory of "art as a game."

III *Structural Aspects of the* Solitudes

Critics of the twentieth century have focused attention on various facets of Góngora's poetic creation, and numerous studies have been turned out on the *Solitudes.* A few of these (apart from the valuable contributions of Dámaso Alonso already discussed) may be briefly summarized in the following fashion:

Walter Pabst was one of the first critics conclusively to demonstrate Góngora's artistic merits in an examination of the language, techniques and "psychology" of the *Solitudes.*[9] His study, originally written in German, may be said to have inaugurated serious foreign study of the poet.

Robert Jammes, a noted French Marxist critic, sees Góngora as the culmination of rebellion against the seventeenth century. Góngora's personal disillusionment with the city and the Court made his protest against the Court and his praise for the rustic life of the country more than just a rehash of the poetic *topos* of the century. Jammes also studies the dominance of sea imagery in the *Solitudes* and its importance in the poem. Most important is the fact that Jammes supports the theory that the *Solitudes* are a form of courtly poetry and that Góngora could not completely free himself from that tradition to the extent that he included the aristocratic pastime of the hunt in the second part. But, of course, the noble gentlemen of the hunt are from the rural aristocracy; the nobility of the province is still superior to that of the Court and the urban areas.[10]

R. O. Jones has shown that the *Solitudes* are more than just a long series of images and metaphors. He sees the work in the context of social commentary, as a vision of the Neoplatonic harmony of the universe, so prevalent in European thought and Renaissance literature, and as a manifestation of the poetic notation of *música mundana* (mundane music). Moreover, Jones explains the violence of the second *Solitude* as disillusion with the world (transience, futility, and death) very much in the manner of Gracián's *Criticón.* For Jones, the central theme of the *Solitudes* is "a praise of the natural life for its own sake."[11]

Eunice Joiner Gates, a prominent Góngora scholar, defines the Baroque as evidenced in the *Polyphemus* and the *Solitudes.* Special reference is made to the plastic arts and to Wölfflin's famous hypothesis. She compares Góngora's poetic technique to such painters as Caravaggio, Ribera, Rubens, El Greco, showing that Góngora made use of the artistic elements that were part of the common heritage of the classical and Renaissance periods.[12]

Emilio Orozco has also made several significant contributions. He has been mainly concerned with some major contemporaneous documents concerning the *Solitudes*, which have been published along with Orozco's annotations. Primarily, he views the *Solitudes* as an expression of Góngora's intimate life—life and literature are but a single fusion of experience. Therefore, the *Solitudes* are biographical and, when Góngora left his solitary life behind, he had no reason to continue with his poem. This then is the reason for the assumedly unfinished composition.[13]

Maurice Molho uses current European theories on semantics to demonstrate how Góngora used words in unique and unexpected ways in the *Solitudes*. Molho provides precise examples of Góngora's original semantic control of his words, which the poet takes beyond normal poetic meaning. This has, of course, been said before: what Molho offers is a detailed demonstration within an explicit theoretical framework.[14]

However, what criticism to date has not offered for the *Solitudes* is a detailed effort to unfold the interrelated threads, the organization or narrative structure of the poem.[15] Indeed, Góngora was a gifted craftsman who, we must assume, consciously ordered a beautiful poetic world of artistic conceit, ambiguity, and philosophical, aesthetic, and social concern. What seems most immediate is the need to see how various major structural devices give the poem a unified, narrative whole, thus making the poem a hermetic world of sound and meaning.

Starting with the dedication, one finds the introduction to the *Solitudes* to be a short dramatic preface wherein Góngora offers a preview for the entire poem. The thirty-seven lines set the tone, mood, and the stage for the composition. The poet, confessing to be at the mercy of the *dulce Musa*, the Gentle Muse, writes from inspiration while realizing the dual fate of his verses: some will live while others are to be lost in "lonely images" just like the footprints of his shipwrecked hero. Thus, Góngora compares the fate of the writer's art to that of his wandering pilgrim hero (who becomes both the poet as well as the protagonist of the work in an excellent example of conceitful *Doppelgängerei;* Molho has commented in particular upon this feature of the dedication.[16] The next eight lines are an invocation to the Duque de Béjar, who is simply addressed as *tú* (thou). The poet appeals to our visual and auditory senses as he describes the dread of the hunt: armed men who encroach upon nature, seeking to kill beasts who "stain the land with red" and "coral froth" on the Tormes.

The next thirteen lines are an intensification of the previous stanza; with a highly detailed account of the tradition of the courtly hunt, the poet implores the Duke to cease the hunt (just as he had requested the Conde de Niebla in the *Polyphemus*). The poet assumes the role of counselor, advising the Duke to rest in the shade of an oak as befits his "godlike eminence." One's attention is drawn to the ancient custom of the hunters hanging their spoils in the oak and pine trees (the bear's head may thus kiss the instrument which killed him).

"Oh Duque esclarecido!" ("Lord of all excellence!") begins the next stanza with the poet addressing his patron. This time as interpreter of nature, he tells the Duke that nature serves and soothes man; thus the Duke is again asked to take his ease and to listen to the harmonious verses which he will sing to him concerning the wandering steps of his hero (who, as suggested above, is the ironic extension of Góngora himself). In retrospect, of course, we realize that a symbol of the court *par excellence* is being enjoined to attend to an anticourtly eulogy—almost an allegory, if you will. Hence the special significance of the request to suspend the courtly hunt and to pay attention to the poem. At this point the author projects himself into his work as he did in the first stanza; apparently the reality created within the literary work is an essential one for Góngora. Thus, there is a circular pattern in the dedication, as the wandering steps of the hero in the first stanza are again repeated in the fourth stanza and are identified with the lines of the poet's lyrics. Everything is tied together, as Góngora's own footsteps along with the lyrics of his poetry and the footsteps of the protagonist have found their way to a very eminent patron. Thus, there is an ingenious interplay between the literal and the figurative, between the poet-wanderer and the protagonist-wanderer.

The last five lines are anticlimactic and elaborate a point of traditional poetic convention of the Renaissance; the poet's promise to give immortal fame to his patron through his lyrics. The poet, imprisoned and bound by patronage, knows that his Muse Euterpe will sing the Duke's praises even when Fame's trumpet has ceased to play. This, of course, reflects the time-honored concept of immortality for mortals through the power of art and literature.

This dedication is really a microcosm of the total composition in that the everpresent plaintive mood is accompanied by the complicated linguistic syntax of hyperbaton, bifurcation (Gracián, Góngora's great mid-seventeenth-century critic, recognized him as the master of this poetic device which abounds in the *Solitudes* and his other works), allusions, myth, and the pagan world of Góngora. The major themes are suggested: the loneliness and alienation of the wanderer and poet, the excitement of the hunt, man as an interloper in Nature and his capacity to disturb the natural order and, in contrast to these, the energy and fertility of Nature. Also, music, death, animals (the bear and beasts), and the physical world of Nature (the huge oak, the pine trees, flowing water, grass) are all part of the cast of the entire drama. There is the pervasive sensitivity for color as well as the strong nominal style (Góngora paid particular creative attention to nouns and nominalizations) and in the dedication alone sixty-four nouns appear.[17] All these features prepare the groundwork for the spectacle which is about to commence in the main body of the poem. In addition, one notes Góngora's love for a climactic end, followed by postclimax to reemphasize his poetic commentary. Indeed, the dedication serves a special function, that of a miniature poem, an abstract of the larger composition.

It is significant that Góngora opens his poem in reflective recollection by remembering that "Era del año la estación florida ("It was the flowery season of the year"). It is springtime—the energetic season of rebirth, innocence, and youth—and the passive *náufrago* or shipwrecked youth (who is physically alienated from the land and emotionally estranged from his beloved) enters a new world. The shipwreck and its trauma occasion a fresh consciousness, the challenge to formulate an original experience. In fact, the youth represents a *homo viator* who is to wander and to search and to discover an alternate world. This is primarily the broader framework of the poem. Immediately, in the first stanza Góngora makes use of anthropopathia in his constant personification of the Nature that represents another principal actor in his dramatic narrative; Nature is always in the state of becoming and feeling like a human being. Throughout the poem, Nature is personified; moreover pathetic fallacy is a thread which frequently ties the various stanzas together. For instance, in the first *Solitude* the rejected lover weeps in such a way that he moves the winds and the waves, thus causing the ocean to take pity on him to save his life by washing him ashore (ll. 10–14). In the second *Solitude,* in parallel fashion, one notes again the sweet lament of one of the fishermen, and here the waves stop to listen and the rocks cry with pity (ll. 38–40). At the same point, Góngora reveals in the first stanza what he will do throughout the entire composition. There is a fusion of time, and the narrative voice speaks in both the present and the past tense to describe a given situation. Perhaps this procedure should be understood to indicate that Góngora, so absorbed in his role as a skilled narrator, is unhampered by time and tense. In other words, his is an awareness of multiple levels of existence, a consciousness of past via memory as well as the ideas and sensations of the very precious present moment which form the total unity of experience. Involved in recollection, Góngora introduces the present moment wherein Taurus *is* grazing upon the star (evidently it is late afternoon in the month of April) and the rejected lover *is* weeping. One frequently can identify this system of shifting tenses within the same sentence as he reads the *Solitudes;* in fact, most of the stanzas contain this poetic use of time both to make time real and then to distort it, making it unreal.

Parallel to the first *Solitude,* the second *Solitude* also sets the scene within a marine-type setting, and likewise, there is a smooth continuity between the two poetic movements in that there is no interruption of time. Góngora follows a classical approach whereby the action of both *Solitudes* is compressed into a brief period of time. The first *Solitude* spans three calendar days, beginning in late afternoon and ending in the evening two days later. The second *Solitude* has a trajectory of two days, beginning the morning after the wedding and breaking off suddenly the next day with the afternoon hunt. And as regards the classical orientation of literary creation, Góngora poses an Aristotelian problem with his work, for he presents the stormy sea of life as his subject matter in the first *Solitude.* That is, there must follow from this "action" the working out of the tragic situation of his protagonist. Also, Góngora chooses to present action in the more traditional narrative sense since there is a sequential patterning of events and happenings in linear progression. The first *Solitude* projects the arrival of the shipwrecked youth, the meeting with the goatherd, the wedding procession, the old man's discourse, wedding festivities, the wedding and the athletic contests, and finally the newlyweds' retirement to their abode. The second *Solitude* relates the trip to the tiny isle, the visit with the fisherman and his daughters, the old man's account of his daughters' fishing prowess, the melancholy laments of Lycidas and Micón, followed by the hunt.

Another major cornerstone of Góngora's systematic structure is his use of the protagonist as *Aussenseiter*-spy. A paramount structural device which holds the poem together is this youth who is always *witnessing, observing,* or *spying* upon the action as an outsider. This procedure provides a bridge between the purely pastoral world of the poem and the courtly world of the reader from where the *náufrago* comes.

But it is the treatment of narrative voice that dominates the structure of the *Solitudes.* Most interesting is that the poetic voice is always that of the poet. This means that the poet speaks, describes, interprets, and quotes what the various characters say. Góngora constantly strives to impose *his* style. In the first *Solitude,* just after applying sea imagery to the countryside (a poetic constant), the narrator says:

> *farol de una cabaña*
> *que sobre el ferro está, en aquel incierto*
> *golfo de sombras anunciando el puerto.* (ll. 59–61)[18]
> (A cottage lamp maybe—
> An anchored beacon, piercing from afar
> These shadowy gulfs, to mark the harbour bar.[19])

The poetic voice makes a quick transition by arresting the action by directly quoting what the protagonist says:

> *«rayos—les dice—ya que no de Leda*
> *trémulos hijos, sed de mi fortuna*
> *término luminoso.»* (ll. 62–64)
> ("O rays, if not the mocking fire," he cried,
> Of Leda's sons, in you my woes may find
> A luminous conclusion!")

And then the poetic voice turns its attention to a description of Nature, which this time could be a forbidding, rugged, jealous

Nature, unreceptive to the presence of the interloper protagonist.

In contrast, a few lines later, upon finding his way and newfound friends among the goatherds, the shipwrecked victim draws attention with a refreshing initiative by singing an encomium to the *beatus ille* (blessed is he [who tills the soil]). Stanzas 8, 9, and 10 of the first *Solitude* are the only lines employing exclamation marks. (But, conversely, the exclamatory mode occurs more frequently in the second *Solitude*, in lines 121–24, 453–54, 571, 618, 626–27, 652–61, 674–76, and 959–60.) These stanzas recapitulate the dominant meaning of the poem, for they elaborate the joys of the simple rustic life; a small segment speaks for the entire poem:

¡Oh bienaventurado
albergue a cualquier hora,
templo de Pales, alquería de Flora!
No moderno artificio
borró designios, bosquejó modelos,
al cóncavo ajustando de los cielos
el sublime edificio;
retamas sobre robre
tu fábrica son pobre,
do guarda, en vez de acero,
la inocencia al cabrero
más que el silbo al ganado.
¡Oh bienaventurado
albergue a cualquier hora!

No en ti la ambición mora
hidrópica de viento
ni la que su alimento
el áspid es gitano;
no la que, en vulto comenzando humano,
acaba en mortal fiera,
esfinge bachillera,
que hace hoy a Narciso
ecos solicitar, desdeñar fuentes;
ni la que en salvas gasta impertinentes
la pólvora del tiempo más preciso:
ceremonia profana
que la sinceridad burla villana
sobre el corvo cayado.

¡Oh bienaventurado
albergue a cualquier hora!

Tus umbrales ignora
la adulación, sirena
de reales palacios, cuya arena
besó ya tanto leño:
trofeos dulces de un canoro sueño.
No a la soberbia está aquí la mentira
dorándole los pies, en cuanto gira
la esfera de sus plumas,
ni de los rayos baja a las espumas
favor de cera alado.
¡Oh bienaventurado
albergue a cualquier hora! (ll. 94–135)

(O fortunate retreat
At whatsoever hour—
A pastoral temple and a floral bower!
No modern artist strove
With studied plan and elevated style
To match in grandeur with the lofty pile
The arching vault above.
Thatch upon oak instead
A modest dwelling made,
Which rural innocence
Bars with a stronger fence
Than sheep-pipe straying feet.
O fortunate retreat
At whatsoever hour!

Here is no lust for power,
No thirst for windy fame;
No envy to inflame
Like Egypt's aspic race;
Nor she who, sphinx-like, wears a human face
Above her bestial loins,
Whose wily voice enjoins
Narcissus' modern seed
To follow Echo, and despise the well;
Nor she whose insolent salvos now dispel
The powder treasured by a thriftier breed.
Propped on his shepherd's crook

Rustic simplicity amused may look
    Upon her courtly cheat.
    O fortunate retreat
    At whatsoever hour!

    From this umbrageous bower
    Flattery's voice is banned,
Siren of royal courts, beneath whose sand
    Many a vessel lies,
Relics of these delusive lullabies.
Here Falsehood does not gild her feet of Pride,
Though she display her feathery circle wide;
    None hurtles seaward here
Whose wax-bound pinions carried him too near
    Favour's deceptive heat.
    O fortunate retreat
    At whatsoever hour!)

The poetic voice asserts itself through the protagonist's song, whose immediate audience is both that of the goatherds who are listening as well as the literary audience, an interesting juxtaposition, whereby the reader is drawn into participation. From the outset, one notes the *stylus gravis* used to describe the life of the peasant. *No* is the word which joins the series of ideas, ideas which reflect the negative values of the court as opposed to the positive virtues of the country. Most important here (and in other parts of the poem) is how the poetic voice, in an active or passive role, uses courtly language to express the noncourtly. There are three stanzas device of declaring what *does not* exist in order to express what that relate what the quiet retreat is *not*, using Góngora's favorite device of declaring what *does not* exist in order to express what *does* exist. The exclamatory elaboration insists that the quiet retreat is *not* a place beautified by art and architecture, but rather a place of rural innocence with modest dwellings. It is *not* a place where weapons are needed (as at court), since innocence protects the shepherd. The contrast *campo* vs. *corte* is intensified by Góngora's lofty, poetic language used to describe the country as he continues to sing behind the mask of the protagonist. The ninth stanza follows in this most intense mode, and the rejection of the court is stronger. The country is *not* ambition or envy or lasciviousness or formal ceremony. The more viable realities of the pastoral life are even more evident, for the peasant is a superior creature who can even laugh in comfort at the empty life of the court. The tenth stanza reinforces the greatness of the rustic setting by naming other vices of the court, such as flattery, falsehood, and the fall of favorites and the powerful. The rhythm of the stanzas are free-flowing, for there is no use of fixed stanzaic structure, a characteristic of the *silva.* The famous refrain "O fortunate retreat/at whatsoever hour!" recurs to open and close the eighth and tenth stanzas and emphasizes the theme of the song as well as that of the whole work.

The castaway's song extends into the second *Solitude.* But, instead of an encomium, his objective commentary gives way to a *métrico llanto* (metric plaint), filled with subjective melancholy and gloomy thoughts of death. This is striking counterpoint to the earlier *beatus ille* and at the same time it is parallel with the first *Solitude* (ll. 737–42) where his thoughts dwell upon his personal misfortune and misery. This *llanto* begins on line 116 (almost in the same position as in the first *Solitude* (and consists of eight stanzas. This time the sea is the youth's audience, as he recounts the tragedy of his wanderings, his unrequited love, and his alienation for five years both on land and sea. This plaintive song serves as a repetitive summary of all that has been told in the poem before with one dimension added, the death wish of the protagonist and his desire to be buried at sea.

This poetic voice is uniform in both *Solitudes* no matter whom the poet is quoting. Parallel discourses in each of the two parts provide symmetry in the work. In the first *Solitude* the old man's discourse of seven stanzas (starting on line 366) combines tones of excitement and disenchantment and realism in his denunciation of Spain's commercialism, greed, and seafaring which break the natural and moral order. The young wanderer listens as he does in the second *Solitude* during the speech of the aged fisherman (ll. 355–510). Both speakers are fathers and humble, old men; both use elegant expression, abundant metaphor as well as mythological and historical references. Their maturity has been blessed with a broad perspective as they focus their attention on the sea and its capacity for rebellion and violence. Yet their frame of reference is different. The old man of the first *Solitude* stresses the evils of the sea (he has lost a son to it) as well as the evils of man's perversion of nature by his conquest of the seas. The old man in the second *Solitude* is a more temperate soul with a positive vision of the sea. The sea is a friend, obedient to the needs of the man who lives from the sea (his sons and daughters show great prowess on the sea and in counterpoint to the first discourse, the use of the sea for personal livelihood is acceptable to Góngora).

Another dimension of the narrative voice is seen when Góngora projects himself into the poem. As already noted, he did this in the dedication. Upon winding things up in a somewhat circular pattern, he uses *Yo* in the second *Solitude*. With *yo lo dudo* (I doubt it), line 778, he does not bother to suppress his own voice as he comments on the indomitability of the hawk. In this way, Góngora effects an identity between himself as a person and himself as a lyric *persona*.

It may said that the poet Góngora assumes many guises in the *Solitudes:* poet, protagonist/wanderer, old men, chorus, rustic maidens, and plaintive youth. Moreover, the narrative or poetic voice encompasses two situations, that of storyteller and that of the drama which he narrates. In spite of the different characters who appear in the poem, we only hear a single voice, presumably Góngora's. But this single voice changes in point of view and tone: hyperbolic descriptions of nature, objective narration of the hunt, exuberant encomium, joyous song of invocation, subjective and plaintive song, disenchanted versus temperate discourse.

IV *Dramatic Structure in the* Solitudes

The narrative voice also assumes another function of structure in the *Solitudes,* that of drama or dramatic design. For, indeed, Góngora was conscious of the concept of theater in the work. The dramatic framework of the poem is significant in that each stanza dramatizes the exterior physical world of Nature and at times penetrates the interior world of the protagonist or other characters. Drama, therefore, is a structural matter in the Solitudes with the presence of several dramatic elements: asides, spoken or sung dialogue, instrumental and vocal music, dance, color, exoticism, pageantry, dramatic contrast, and even a consciousness of the word *teatro.* It is especially these elements of drama which give unity to the poem.

The profusion of asides functions not only to heighten dramatic movement, but to personalize strongly the *Solitudes* to the extent that the reader is assured that the lyrics are definitely addressed to him; the dramatic nature of the asides goes beyond plot and character to establish intimate contact with the reader. The latter always receives Góngora's extended interpretation on some aspect of life whether it be concerning the specific nature of love or a passing comment on some phenomenon observed. In the first *Solitude,* upon mentioning the "Arabian bird" (the Phoenix, in line 462), he comments that its flight emulates a rainbow in the sky. In the second *Solitude,* he speaks about streamlets in terms of the gliding of a snake—but, he assures the reader, a streamlet vomits a spray of pearls (water) instead of poison. Over and over again we have such asides which strengthen tension and imagination in the verses.

R.O. Jones has discussed the importance of music and harmony in the *Solitudes* in terms of Neoplatonism. It is music which heightens the aesthetic experience by changing the dramatic situation into different moods involving magic, eroticism, religiousness, and the pleasure of inspiration. Throughout the composition, the unifying agent of music, instrumental or vocal, recurs often as a major motif which deepens the sensory and artistic impact.

Góngora's artfulness prepares the stage for the choral group's invocation to the pagan god Hymen, who is beseeched to bless the wedded ones. The poet/speaker frames the pastoral background of the stage wherein all of mankind functions as the chorus which in Greek fashion participates and comments upon the action—here, more specifically the wedding. *Ven, Himeneo . . .* ("Come, Hymen . . .") opens and closes each of the six stanzas (ll. 780–844). The first chorus is comprised of enchanting maidens, while the second chorus consists of the shepherds; this is a litany-type prayer filled with sensual imagery. For instance, lines 801–04:

> *mudos coronen otros por su turno*
> *el dulce lecho conyugal, en cuanto*
> *lasciva abeja al virginal acanto*
> *néctar le chupa hibleo.*
> (The nuptial couch let others mutely keep
> Where, like the avid bee, the bridegroom sips
> Hyblean nectar from her virgin lips
> Rivaling acanthine red.)

The change of voices as well as point of view offer counterbalance; the overtones are religious in an erotic, pagan sense. The maidens ask for blessings of a more material nature, blessings for the bridal pair, the bridal bed, and the bridal store (in terms of material plenty and the birth of "sturdy sons"); while the males request blessings that tend to be more abstract, the bridal day, the bridal bond, and the bridal vow. Simultaneously, the *culto himno* (learned hymn) elaborates the themes of bountiful nature, and the happiness and harmony of marriage.

This dramatic song continues in parallel fashion in lines 893–943 when the rustic maidens sing their wishes for the couple. Two features are important. First is the correspondence of mood between the two lyrical songs—the use of optative subjunctives in both describes the ideal state that the human condition wishes to attain. The musical lyrics render a description not of *what is,* but of what life *should be.* In the second wedding song, more dramatic action occurs when the pastoral stage is enhanced with the graceful dancing of twelve maidens, nymphs who open and close the song in dance. What is more, the poetic voice makes an observation which could serve as an epithet to the whole poem:

> *entró bailando numerosamente;*
> *y dulce musa entre ellas—si consiente*
> *bárbaras el Parnaso moradoras—* (ll. 890–92)
> (In rhythmic dance, among them one who might
> Be thought a Muse, did the Parnassian height
> Such rustic dwellers on its slopes allow.)

Such is the glory of the rustic life that a Muse may even dwell there, and creativity is to be found in the simple life. The rustic maiden, really a Muse, deserves to be on the Olympus of the gods. This hyperbolic conception underlies the fundamental elevation of the content of the poem via the *stylus gravis.* The marriage celebration, with all the drama of song and dance, embodies the principal action of the first *Solitude* simply because marriage is the reenactment of Nature in pure harmony, the constant birth and rebirth of life.

In contrast to the drama provided by the human beings, there is the spontaneous drama of nature in interaction with humanity. Nature's own music, that of the flowing water of a stream, offers sleep to the travelers (ll. 342–49) of the first *Solitude*. One of the most beautiful passages in the work brings into sharp focus the drama of man and Nature in perfect harmony, caught up in the inimitable rhythm of music and song: in lines 54–61, the mountain sirens engage in alternate song while *Pintadas aves . . . cítaras de pluma* ("Songbirds, like feathered lyres, in plumage gay") are enraptured with the rustic chorus while the streamlet listens attentively. And in lines 585–86, the concert of crystal water, the *músicas hojas* (the melodious foliage) along with the wind and birds form a part of the dramatic pageantry, weaving a magical world of color and sound which casts a spell on the fictional spectator (the wanderer) as well as on the literary spectator. A sense of passion, movement, tension are expierenced by Nature, the peasants, and the audience.

This same ritual of music and drama unfolds in a similar manner in the second *Solitude*, but the subsequent rhythm, here, however, falls to a crescendo. Zest and enthusiasm become seriousness and melancholy. The spontaneous naturalness of the drama changes to a more philosophical contemplation. The youth's song (ll. 112–71) is not an encomium to life but rather a thoughtful assessment of his plight as disdained lover and estranged victim. No longer is there the revelry, dancing and movement, nor the feeling of kinship. The tone is restrained and formal and the "silent spongy sea" acts as the audience. And again Góngora sets the stage: the boat is the youth's zither, and the oars his strings.

Yet one notes a tie with the first *Solitude* in that music and Nature represent the principal actors in this drama of world harmony. Lines 349–60 of the second *Solitude* almost exactly parallel the setting, theme, mood, and spectacle of lines 550–61 of the first *Solitude* to the extent that the lyrics seem to be a form of the same melody, sound, and color:

Rompida el agua en las menudas piedras,
cristalina sonante era tiorba,
y las confusamente acordes aves,
entre las verdes roscas de las yedras,
muchas eran, y muchas veces nueve
aladas musas, que—de pluma leve
engañada su oculta lira corva—
metros inciertos sí, pero süaves,

en idiomas cantan diferentes;
mientras, cenando en pórfidos lucientes,
lisonjean apenas
al Júpiter marino tres sirenas. (ll. 349–60)
(The water, eddying round the tiny stones,
Played on a crystalline theorbo's strings;
Among the ivy's verdant coils there rang
The birds' confused and yet harmonious tones;
Many they were, and many times their choirs
Surpassed the nine winged Muses—curving lyres
Disguised beneath their lightly feathered wings—
And sweetly, if uncertainly, they sang
Each in his diverse tongue; while in the sea
Supping on thrones of lucent porphyry,
Three sirens vainly strove
To please the ear of ocean-ruling Jove.)

This appears to be an identical scene of the same act. Harmony exists; the chorus of maidens in the first *Solitude* is complimented by the chorus of birds in the second poem (they recall the *pintadas aves*), but the latter sing in different tongues while the wanderer dines with his friends. And as an objective correlative of human activity, Neptune dines under the sea while listening to the music of three sirens. This scene presents a striking drama of the court (the humble court of the fisherman and his family versus the legendary one of Neptune), but the pageantry lies within the realm of the natural world, in this case, the sea.

By juxtaposition, one witnesses a more stylized drama in the second *Solitude*. In ten stanzas (ll. 542–611), Lycidas and Micón sing an artistic barcarole. The lyrics suggest a rowing rhythm in correlation with the actual feat of their rowing a boat as they sing. Again, the sea acts as a point of reference, for the lament of the lovelorn fishermen (this lament, also a *llanto métrico,* parallels the protagonist's lament at the start of the second *Solitude*. They too view the sea as their possible tomb, but their love will be fulfilled in contrast to the unrequited love that the protagonist has experienced. Their song is a dialogue that is sung; it is a dramatic encounter in which each young man answers the other while the audience—the protagonist and his friends, their father and the daughters—even Night and Cupid—all feel a catharsis. The fishermen in the expression of their agony and the audience (the literary audience included) are deeply stirred by such love and sentiment. This beautiful barcarole represents another example of Góngora's oral/aural/dramatic commitment in poetry.

Other points of drama thread their way throughout the *Solitudes:* the drama of the fisherman's account regarding the fishing skills of his daughters parallels the drama of the hunt. Nature herself is a dramatic character who exerts herself with many moods in both poetic movements, with their endless references to the seas, rivers, shores, islands, mountains (*locus amoenus* and *beatus ille*), insects, fish, flowers, food, wine, bees, birds, exotic and domestic animals, and brilliant colors of all hues. Góngora's vision of poetry as knowledge is itself a drama, academic drama at its best as he alludes to an abundance of historical allusions (seventy-two references in the first *Solitude;* sixty-seven in the second; added to these one finds allusions to mythology (195 in the first *Solitude* and 138 in the second).[20]

Furthermore, Góngora incorporates the concept of theater within his poetic world. In the first *Solitude* he sees the magnificent girls as actresses who charm and delight in the "confined and peaceful scene": *Mezcladas hacen todas/teatro dulce* ("The girls, all mixed together, made a pleasant theatre"; ll. 623–24). Later, in line 981, he refers to the theatrical spectacle of the athletic contest, mentioning the physical setting of the theater, "When only two-thirds of the theater was lit up by the sun." And in the second *Solitude,* one notes a consciousness of theater when the aged fisherman describes the sea (the metaphor of life) as *ese teatro de Fortuna* ("Fortune's theater"; line 401).

Within the framework of the poetic drama, the underlying narrative tag of the *Solitudes* may be identified as *pues* (thus). What is curious is that the word is such a common connective and represents a startling contrast to Góngora's otherwise carefully chosen vocabulary which he uses for maximum affective purpose. The poet as storyteller handles transitions, digressions, contrasts, as well as a sundry collection of events by giving some order to his poetic creation by use of *pues.* For instance, in the first *Solitude* (ll. 737–38), as the protagonist observes the beautiful bride, his sad past haunts him: *Este, pues, Sol a olvido lo condena . . .* ("That Sun who doomed him once by her disdain . . ."). *Pues* serves here as a connective with the past and at the same time leads to the present image of melancholy and anguish. Or in the second *Solitude* (ll. 343–48), Góngora moves from the meticulous descriptive detail of the exquisite linen tablecloths woven by the fair maidens—and then to change the subject in order to advance the action, he uses *pues:* "then they all sat down to the meal."

The word *pues* plays a marked role in the linear development of the plot: this happened, then this, and then this. It is indeed a key by which the poet controls and moves the action, sets the stage, describes the scenery, changes moods, effects contrasts, introduces characters and dialogue.

The *Solitudes* clearly reject the traditional mimetic concept of poetry in favor of a pragmatic vision of art. That is, Góngora does not believe that art should be an imitation of life, but rather he embraces the quasi-didactic view that life should strive to approximate art. Upon telling the Duke to suspend the hunt and to attend his poem, Góngora initiates a work which offers a pastoral alternative to the courtly life represented by the Duke and the hunt. For this reason, an understanding of the structural aspects of the poem which go towards creating that "pragmatic" artistic whole—"poetic world"—adds still another dimension to the much studied stylistic and linguistic features of the work.

CHAPTER 6

Conclusions

IN discussing criticism on the *Solitudes*, we had occasion to refer to Dámaso Alonso's retrospective statement concerning Góngora's work, a statement born of four decades of close and analytical work with the poet's texts. That statement in effect argues that despite the Cordoban's undeniable technical brilliance, Alonso, a poet himself, was forced to confess that he saw Góngora lacking today in profound human sentiment. Alonso's statement, which is a subjective personal assessment that nevertheless commands attention as coming from the dean of Góngora scholars, is telling and cannot be argued away. Indeed, any honest summation must face up to its essential validity. Thus, while the author of a critical study on Quevedo, Góngora's remarkable contemporary, can refer to aspects of a more current interest such as the poet as witness to a world on the verge of dissolution and prefigurations of present-day black and scatological humor, little immediate appeal to midtwentieth-century intellectual and cultural concerns is likely in the case of Góngora.

Of course, we have not pursued a primarily thematic analysis of Góngora's works, although we have referred to Robert Jammes' massive thematic study—the interesting, if not always engaging, attempt by a Marxist critic to see reflected in the works of the poet a rebellious denunciation of the class in power and their values in his own age. Our own study, which attempts to inquire into structural and technical aspects of the poetry, cannot, nevertheless, avoid the discussion of content. And as we have argued, one of the overriding bases of structural unity in the apparently formless *Solitudes* is the elaboration of a world and a value system that are to "supplant" that from which the shipwrecked protagonist has fled: the power-centered court.

But then all of this seems to be somewhat in a minor key when compared to Quevedo's equally rebellious but differently-phrased version of human existence as seen in terms of seventeenth-century Spain. Góngora's continued adherence to a pastoral-Arcadian landscape, whether the prefabricated mythological one of the *Polyphemus* or the abstract contemporaneous one of the *Solitudes,* will unquestionably strike the reader of agressive "relevancies" as lamentably escapist. The critic has no good defense against such a line of thinking—or of evaluating—even where that critic may accept in other contexts the argument in favor of a demand for relevancies, etc. The question is the extent to which the reader is willing to accept the self-defined relevancies postulated by serious literature as well as his ability to accept a worth for literature on the basis of factors other than gross, reductionary content.

That Góngora was a poet of serious intentions is undeniable. That he was concerned with and fascinated by certain facets of human nature and the human condition is demonstrable. Some of his compositions may be frivolous or be the self-indulgences of a brilliant verbal acrobat. Some of them may be sincere but unsuccessful examples of the poet "at work." Yet despite whatever cavillings one may have over certain of Góngora's works for either their occasional nature or their lack of an agressive "commitment," the poet's reputation is firmly established. One might well ask why, given these frequent negative positions and given the presence of the more "acceptable" content of a Quevedo.

The eulogies over language are, to be sure, a sufficient justification of the poet's accomplishments, although present-day poetry may, again, well prefer a different modality. But seen as the culmination of attempts beginning in the Middle Ages, but pursued with particular vigor and talent in the Renaissance and Baroque, to forge an acceptable vernacular poetic language, Góngora's significance for the definitive establishment of Spanish as a means of literary expression is unquestionable. Ironically, however, for many of his contemporaries and for most modern readers, it is precisely the linguistic vehicle, a unique welding of lexical and syntactic features, which is the greatest hindrance to getting at the poet's "meaning." But one must understand that Góngora's classical, literary Spanish, like classical, literary Latin, is conceived of as a singularly noncolloquial and self-conscious language, the comprehension of which necessarily excludes all but the initiated. The critic must demand that the reader appreciate this elitist conception of poetry—to repeat, the outgrowth of a deliberate attempt to challenge the supremacy of classical Latin—although he cannot easily demand that the modern reader accept it. Indeed, perhaps for many (but not Jammes, one will recall, who barely mentions language) the particular conception of the nature of literary language and, as a necessary consequence, of the function and audience of literature, will vitiate any truly human content otherwise discoverable in Góngora's poems. But then this is a controversy which is four hundred years old, and no easy response to the skeptic is possible—or permissible.

For our purposes, it has been enough to show that there is an identifiable "content" to Góngora's works, one which is closely related to an overall Baroque uneasiness toward the potential perfection and happiness of man as preached by Christian morals and ethics. To be sure, Góngora may couch his conception of the human circumstance in abstract mythological or ideological terms. But as we have argued for the two long compositions, the narrative abstractions do suggest a way out of the bleakness of the contemporary Counter-Reformation world: the "salvation" through art in the *Polyphemus* and the "salvation" through a return to the Golden Mean of an Arcadian existence in the *Solitudes*. Beyond this and beyond the well-studied stylistic contributions—which have been so important to contemporary Spanish poetry—the particular realization of complex structural patterns is a further attribute of Góngora's accomplishments. As in Booth's discussion of Shakespeare's sonnets, these patterns are aesthetically satisfying, functional in terms of a necessary artistic unity, and vital to the effective organization of a poetic vision. To whatever extent the critic must concern himself with these patterns as a fundamental aspect of literary art, our study has underlined them as additional witness to Góngora's contributions to the literature of the seventeenth century.

Notes and References

Chronology

1. It should be noted that the poet's name should be Luis de Argote (patronymic) [y] Góngora (matronymic). The process of inversion, to give Góngora y Argote, is not infrequent when the matronymic is more favored.

Chapter One

1. The best sources of biographical data are Miguel Artigas, *Don Luis de Góngora y Argote. Biografía y estudio crítico* (Madrid: Real Academia Española, 1925); and Dámaso Alonso, *Góngora y el «Polifemo»*. 5th ed. (Madrid: Gredos, 1967).
2. For a discussion of these trends see Lucien-Paul Thomas, *Góngora et le gongorisme considérés dans leurs rapports avec le marinisme* (Paris: H. Champion, 1911); and Andrée Collard, *Nueva poesía: conceptismo, culteranismo en la crítica española* (Madrid: Castalia, 1967). For a rather irreverent discussion see Elisha K. Kane, *Gongorism and the Golden Age* (Chapel Hill: University of North Carolina Press, 1928). See also the first volume of Alonso's study, *Góngora y el «Polifemo»*.
3. Concerning the medieval legacy of both tendencies of the Baroque, see Ernst Robert Curtius' discussion of "Mannerism" (his term for the Baroque) in his *European Literature and the Latin Middle Ages* (New York: Pantheon, 1953), Chapter 15.
4. See the many examples given in Dámaso Alonso's studies; in particular in *La lengua poética de Góngora*. 3d. ed. (Madrid: Consejo Superior de Investigaciones Científicas, 1961).
5. Volume I of Dámaso Alonso, *Góngora y el «Polifemo»*, pp. 59–94, focuses on Góngora's legacy, as does his *Estudios y ensayos gongorinos*. 3d. ed. (Madrid: Gredos, 1970), especially pp. 421–508.
6. Concerning the reevaluation of Góngora and other Baroque poets in the twentieth century, see Elsa Dehennin, *La résurgence de Góngora et la génération poétique de 1927* (Paris; Didier, 1962), and the passing references in Emilia de Zuleta, *Historia de la crítica española contemporánea* (Madrid; Gredos, 1966).
7. Don Francisco de Quevedo y Villegas, *Obras completas* (Madrid; Aguilar, 1960), II, 439.
8. The translation is our own.

9. Quevedo, p. 441.

10. The translation is from Elías L. Rivers, *Renaissance and Baroque Poetry of Spain* (New York: Dell, 1966), pp. 304–5.

11. Lope de Vega, *Obras escogidas* (Madrid: Aguilar, 1966), II, 277.

12. The translation is our own.

13. C. C. Smith, "On the Use of Spanish Theoretical Works in the Debate on Gongorism," *Bulletin of Hispanic Studies,* 39 (1962), 165.

14. Eunice Joiner Gates, "Sidelights on Contemporary Criticism of Gongora's *Polifemo*," *PMLA*, 75 (1960), 508.

15. From Eunice Joiner Gates, *Documentos gongorinos* (Mexico: El Colegio de Mexico, 1960), p. 20.

16. See Helmut Hatzfeld, *Estudios sobre el barroco* (Madrid: Gredos, 1964), and Dámaso Alonso, *Góngora y el «Polifemo»,* I.

17. For the relationship of Gracián's theoretical writings to Baroque literary expression, see Virginia Ramos Foster, "A Note on Gracián's *Agudeza y arte de ingenio* and Baroque Esthetics," *Romance Notes,* 11 (1969), 611–16.

18. For a discussion of Wölfflin's principles in Baroque Spanish literature, see Darnell Higgens Roaten and F. Sánchez Escribano, *Wölfflin's Principles on Spanish Drama: 1500–1700* (New York: Hispanic Institute in the United States, 1952). One should note, however, that the Roaten-Sánchez Escribano study has not been unanimously acclaimed.

Chapter Two

1. See the distribution by genre and date of Góngora's works in Oreste Frattoni, *Góngora* (Buenos Aires: Centro Editor de América Latina, 1968), p. 15. There is no general study of the ballads, although Robert Jammes devotes an extensive chapter to them in his *Études sur l'oeuvre de don Luis de Góngora y Argote* (Bordeaux: Institut d'Études Ibériques et Ibéro-Américaines de l'Université de Bordeaux, 1967), pp. 351–465.

2. C. S. Lewis, *The Discarded Image, an Introduction to Medieval and Renaissance Literature* (Cambridge: At the University Press, 1964).

3. Otis Green, *Spain and the Western Tradition* . . . (Madison: University of Wisconsin Press, 1963–66). 4 vols. See vol. I in particular.

4. This ballad—too long for us to consider here—is one of the few that have attracted any extensive critical attention. See A. Terry, "An Interpretation of Góngora's «Fábula de Píramo»," *Bulletin of Hispanic Studies,* 4 (1956), 202–17.

5. See David William Foster, *The Early Spanish Ballad* (New York: Twayne, 1972).

6. Frattoni, p. 31.

7. This is one of Robert Jammes' central points of departure in his study cited in note 1.

8. See Bruce W. Wardropper's study of the variants, "'La más bella niña,'" *Studies in Philology*, 63 (1966), 661–76.

9. Millé, no. 3–1580. (See the last paragraph of our Preface for the citation of texts.)

10. The translation is our own.

11. Dámaso Alonso, *La lengua poética de Góngora*. 3d. ed. corregida (Madrid: Consejo Superior de Investigaciones Científicas, 1961), Cap. IV, "Repetición de Fórmulas Estilísticas."

12. See Karl Vossler, *La poesía de la soledad en España* (Buenos Aires: Losada, 1946).

13. Such addresses to a mythological figure are in turn given support by the religious tradition of the prayer to the maternal figure of chaste, Christian love: "Hail Mary, full of grace . . ."

14. Dámaso Alonso, for example, in the introduction to *La lengua poética*, pp. 21–37. These comments are reproduced in his introduction to an edition of the poem, *Romance de Angélica y Medoro* (Madrid: Aries, 1963).

15. See Edward M. Wilson's general—and rather vague—comments on the poem in "On Góngora's *Angélica y Medoro*," *Bulletin of Hispanic Studies*, 30 (1953), 85–94.

16. Our text is Dámaso Alonso's edition quoted in note 14. Cf. Millé, no. 48–1602.

17. The translation is our own.

18. See Renato Roggioli, "The Oaten Flute," in James R. Calderwood and Harold E. Toliver, eds., *Perspectives on Poetry* (New York: Oxford University Press, 1968), pp. 224–42.

19. Wilson, p. 93.

20. *Poems of Góngora*, selected, introduced, and annotated by R. O. Jones (Cambridge: At the University Press, 1966), pp. 18–20.

21. Millé, no. 23–1587.

22. The translation is our own.

23. We have not been able to examine A. R. Rodríguez, "Una antigua y bella variante del romance de Góngora: «Servía en Orán al Rey»," *Revista del Ateneo*, 5 (1928), 10–14. We might note here that Ramón Menéndez Pidal saw two separate divisions, one Moorish in a strict sense and one "on African and captive themes"; "Servía en Orán . . ." thus would fall into the second group. This, however, has not been a widely accepted distinction (although many of Góngora's ballads do stand out for the presence of the theme of the captive—an extension, to be sure, of the "prisoner of love" topos); see Jammes, pp. 376–77 on this question. One other important ballad on the captive theme is the barcarole, "Amarrado a un duro barco" ("Tied to a Harsh Ship"), Millé, no. 12–1583.

24. Millé, no. 52–1603.

25. The translation is from J. M. Cohen, ed., *The Penguin Book of Spanish Verse;* rev. ed. (Baltimore: Penguin Books, 1960), pp. 222–24, and is quoted with the permission of the publisher.

26. See Dámaso Alonso, *Poesía de la Edad Media y poesía de tipo tradicional* (Madrid: Signo, 1935).

27. In this regard, see Arthur Terry, "The Continuity of Renaissance Criticism; Poetic Theory in Spain Between 1535 and 1650," *Bulletin of Hispanic Studies*, 31 (1954), 27–36. Jammes, p. 446, implicitly supports the applicability of this assertion to "En los pinares de Xúcar" when he claims that this ballad prefigures the *Soledades*, surely the most "objective" poetry of the Spanish Baroque.

28. Concerning the practice of interior duplication, see Leon Livingstone, "Interior Duplication and the Problem of Form in the Modern Spanish Novel," *PMLA*, 73 (1958), 393–406.

29. Concerning parallelistic poetry in Spain, see Eugenio Asensio, "La poética del paralelismo," in his *Poética y realidad en el Cancionero peninsular de la Edad Media* (Madrid: Gredos, 1957), pp. 75–132.

30. Cf. his comments on the poem in *Góngora y el «Polifemo»*, 5th ed. (Madrid: Gredos, 1967), II, 48–49.

Chapter Three

1. Statistical information is provided by Oreste Frattoni, *Góngora* (Buenos Aires: Centro Editor de América Latina, 1968), p. 15.

2. Robert Jammes, *Études sur l'oeuvre poétique de don Luis de Góngora y Argote* (Bordeaux: Institut d'Études Ibériques et Ibéro-Américaines de l'Université de Bordeaux, 1967), p. 365.

3. See, for example, Dámaso Alonso's passing references in "La correlación en la poesía de Góngora," in his *Estudios y ensayos gongorinos*. 3d. ed. (Madrid: Gredos, 1970), pp. 222–47.

4. E. Brockhaus, *Gongoras Sonettendichtung* (Bochum-Langerdreer: H. Pöppinghaus, 1935). The translations for the categories are our own.

5. Running commentaries of a not very inspired nature are also provided by Oreste Frattoni in his brief *Ensayo para una historia del soneto en Góngora* (Buenos Aires: Universidad Nacional de Buenos Aires, Facultad de Filosofía y Letras, 1948). See also the study by Orozco Díaz of some of the sonnets (none of which is discussed in this chapter) within the framework of some highly interesting observations on Mannerism and Baroque: "Estructura manierista y estructura barroca en la poesía. Introducción y comentarios a unos sonetos de Góngora," in *Historia y estructura de la obra literaria* (Madrid: Consejo Superior de Investigaciones Científicas, 1971), pp. 97–115.

6. Concerning the Italian sources and inspiration of Góngora's poetry,

see J. P. W. Crawford, "Italian Sources of Góngora's Poetry," *Romanic Review*, 20 (1929), 122–30; and Joseph G. Fucilla, *Estudios sobre el petrarquismo en España* (Madrid: Consejo Superior de Investigaciones Científicas, 1960), pp. 252–57.

7. See Dámaso Alonso's comments on these relationships in "Garcilaso, Ronsard, Góngora (apuntes de una clase)," in his *De los siglos oscuros al de oro* (Madrid: Gredos, 1958), pp. 183–91. A. Carballo Picazo, "El soneto «Mientras por competir con tu cabello» de Góngora," *Revista de filología española*, 47 (1964), 379–98, provides a thorough analysis of the sources, themes, etc., of the sonnet.

8. Millé, no. 228–1581. Dámaso Alonso has argued for a somewhat different reading for the first quatrain, which we have accepted. See his text in *Góngora y el «Polifemo»*. 5th ed. (Madrid: Gredos, 1967), II, 133–34; and Carballo Picazo's observations on this matter in his article cited in note 7. A recent and excellent edition of the sonnets should be noted: *Sonetos completos;* edición de Biruté Ciplijauskaité (Madrid: Castalia, 1969). See Ciplijauskaité, no. 149, for the text of this sonnet.

9. The translation is our own.

10. See Eugenio Asensio, "La poética del paralelismo," in his *Poética y realidad en el cancionero peninsular de la Edad Media* (Madrid: Gredos, 1957), pp. 75–132.

11. See the reference in note 8.

12. Of course, in Genesis, II, 19, the Latin is *revertaris in terram* [Sp. *tierra*] and *quia pulvis es* [Sp. *polvo*].

13. Millé, no. 238–1584; Ciplijauskaité, no. 70.

14. The translation is our own.

15. For example, G. C. Rossi, "Rileggendo un sonetto di Góngora e uno di Tasso," *Revista de filología española*, 44 (1961), 425–33.

16. Nathan Gross, "Invention in an Imitated Sonnet by Góngora," *Modern Language Notes*, 77 (1962), 182–87; the quote is on pp. 182–83.

17. Stephen Booth, *An Essay on Shakespeare's Sonnets* (New Haven: Yale University Press, 1969).

18. See the discussions of poetic "coupling" by Samuel Levin, *Linguistic Structures in Poetry* (The Hague: Mouton, 1962), Ch. 4.

19. Cf. Gross, pp. 185–87.

20. This latter point is the central thesis of André Collard, *Nueva poesía: conceptismo, culteranismo en la crítica española* (Madrid: Castalia, 1967).

21. Millé, no. 320–1612 [1611]; Ciplijauskaité, no. 138.

22. The translation is our own.

23. *The Poems of Góngora*, selected, introduced and annotated by R. O. Jones (Cambridge: At the University Press, 1966), p. 14.

24. For a discussion of these concepts in Spanish poetry, see David

William Foster, *Christian Allegory and Early Hispanic Poetry* (Lexington, Ky.: The University Press of Kentucky, 1971).

25. One of the meanings of *margarita* in Spanish is "pearl" (note also line 13 for this word in Spanish as *perla*). In premodern Christian symbology, the pearl represented salvation generally and often the Word of God (cf. the Mormon text, *Pearl of Great Price*).

26. Millé, no. 318–1612 [1611]; line 13.

27. See Américo Castro's book on the subject, *Santiago de España* (Buenos Aires: Emecé, 1958).

28. Millé, no. 332–1615 [1614]; Ciplijauskaité, no. 140.

29. The translation is our own.

30. Evelyn Esther Uhrhan, "Linguistic Analysis of Góngora's Baroque Style," in H. R. Kahane, and A. Pietrangeli, *Descriptive Studies in Spanish Grammar* (Urbana: University of Illinois Press, 1954), pp. 177–241.

31. For example, in his *La lengua poética de Góngora*. 3d. ed. corregida (Madrid: Consejo Superior de Investigaciones Científicas, 1961), Capítulo VI, "Hipérbaton."

32. See Booth's evaluation (cf. note 17) of Ransom's criticism, pp. 24 ff.

33. See, in passing, María Rosa Lida's article, "La hipérbole sagrada en la poesía castellana del siglo XV," *Revista de filología hispánica*, 7 (1945), 121–30.

34. Arthur Terry, "The Continuity of Renaissance Criticism: Poetic Theory in Spain Between 1535 and 1650," *Bulletin of Hispanic Studies*, 31 (1954), 27–36.

35. Concerning, in general, Góngora's attitudes toward nature, see Elias L. Rivers, "Nature, Art and Science in Spanish Poetry of the Renaissance," *Bulletin of Hispanic Studies*, 44 (1967), 255–66.

36. Booth, pp. 59–60.

37. See, however, Wilhelm Michel's essay on affinities between Shakespeare and the Spanish Baroque: "Barockstil in Shakespeare und Calderón," *Revue hispanique*, 85 (1929), 370–458.

38. The reader is reminded of three other sonnets that deserve close attention: "¡Oh excelso muro, oh torres coronadas!" ("Oh lofty wall, oh crownèd towers!"), Góngora's famous elegy of Córdoba (Millé, no. 244–1585); "Prisión de nácar era articulado" ("A prison of the mother-of-pearl"), which is purely "decorative" (Millé, no. 357–1620); and "Menos solicitó veloz saeta" ("The speedy arrow demanded less"), another denunciation of the brevity of life and one of the poet's last compositions (Millé, no. 374–1623). The structure of the first sonnet is discussed in detail by Dámaso Alonso, *Estudios y ensayos gongorinos*, pp. 194–97, 231.

39. See the discussion of Santillana's relatively facile sonnets in David William Foster, *The Marqués de Santillana* (New York: Twayne, 1971), Ch. 4.

Chapter Four

1. Concerning these elements of the poem, see Elias L. Rivers, "El conceptismo del *Polifemo*," *Atenea*, No. 363 (1961), 102–9.

2. One of the earliest comprehensive reassessments of Góngora's works, with a concentration on the two long narratives, is Walter Pabst's study, originally published in German, but recently translated into Spanish: *La creación gongorina en los poemas,* Polifemo *y* Soledades (Madrid: Consejo Superior de Investigaciones Científicas, 1966). Of course, Dámaso Alonso has made major contributions to a contemporary understanding of all of Góngora's works, and we will mention several of his studies in documentation of our assertions. In a recent paper, Alonso surveys his major ideas concerning the *Polyphemus:* "El *Polifemo,* poema barroco," *Atenea,* No. 393 (1961), 56–74. The best source of Alonso's ideas on the poem remains his masterly edition of the text, with an accompanying introductory volume and another volume representing an annotated anthology of other compositions: *Góngora y el «Polifemo»* . . . . 5th ed. (Madrid: Gredos, 1967). All quotes from the original Spanish text of the poem are from the third volume of this critical edition.

3. Robert Jammes, *Études sur l'oeuvre poétique de don Luis de Góngora y Argote* (Bordeaux: Institut d'Études Ibériques et Ibéro-Américaines de l'Université de Bordeaux, 1967), Troisième Partie, Chapitre IV. See pp. 564 ff. in particular.

4. We know of no comprehensive study detailing the influence of Ovid's work in Spain. See, however, the sections on the story of Polyphemus and Galatea in José María de Cossío, *Fábulas mitológicas en España* (Madrid: Espasa-Calpe, 1952). Dámaso Alonso discusses in detail the relationship between Góngora's poem, Ovid's original, and other contemporaneous versions of the legend in his article, "La supuesta imitación por Góngora de la «Fábula de Acis y Galatea»," included in his *Estudios y ensayos gongorinos.* 3d. ed. (Madrid: Gredos, 1970), pp. 324–70. The most detailed study of all of the "philological" aspects of the poem remains A. Vilanova's compendium, *Las fuentes y los temas del «Polifemo» de Góngora* (Madrid: Consejo Superior de Investigaciones Científicas, 1957).

5. See in passing Vittorio Bodini's paper, "Góngora e i miti classici," in his *Studi sul Barroco de Góngora* (Roma: Edizioni dell'Ateneo, 1964), pp. 63–77.

6. Dámaso Alonso, "Monstruosidad y belleza en el *Polifemo* de Góngora," in his *Poesía española* . . . (Madrid: Gredos, 1951), pp. 313–92.

7. As defined and described by C. S. Lewis in *The Discard Image* (Cambridge, England: University Press, 1964).

8. This is the current of "amorality"—the lack of a firm commitment to Baroque and/or Counter-Reformation Christian "ideology"—which

Andrée Collard discusses as one major basis for Góngora's tempestuous reception by his contemporaries: *Nueva poesía: conceptismo, culteranismo en la crítica española* (Madrid: Castalia, 1967).

9. R. O. Jones, "Neoplatonism and the *Soledades*," *Bulletin of Hispanic Studies*, 40 (1963), 1–16; and "Góngora and Neoplatonism Again," *Bulletin of Hispanic Studies*, 43 (1966), 117–20.

10. C. Colin Smith, "An Approach to Góngora's *Polifemo*," *Bulletin of Hispanic Studies*, 42 (1965), 217–38. Smith writes specifically against the first of the two Jones articles cited in the preceding note and is answered in turn by the second.

11. Lowry Nelson, Jr., *Baroque Lyric Poetry* (New Haven: Yale University Press, 1961), Part II, Section 4; the quote is from p. 61.

12. See Eunice Joiner Gates, "Góngora's *Polifemo* and *Soledades* in Relation to Baroque Art," *Texas Studies in Literature and Language*, 2 (1960), 61–77. A more comprehensive survey is provided by Darnell H. Roaten, and F. Sánchez Escribano, *Wölfflin's Principles in Spanish Drama: 1500–1700* (New York: Hispanic Institute in the United States, 1952).

13. In addition to Dámaso Alonso's paper cited in note 6, see Oreste Frattoni, "La forma en Góngora. Estudio sobre la dedicatoria del *Polifemo*," in his *La forma en Góngora y otros ensayos* (Rosario, Arg.: Universidad Nacional del Litoral, 1961), pp. 5–16; and Ermanno Caldera "En torno a las tres primeras estrofas del 'Polifemo' de Góngora," in Jaime Sánchez Romeralo, and Norbert Poulussen, *Actas del Segundo Congreso Internacional de Hispanistas* (Nijmegan, Holland: Universidad de Nimega, Instituto Español, 1967), pp. 227–33.

14. See Alonso's elucidation in his critical text, pp. 133–36.

15. A section of Jammes' study is devoted to the sea aspects of the poem and Smith, in his article cited in note 10, also refers to this characteristic. We are using the term "return" in Mircea Eliade's sense of *Le Mythe de l'éternel retour, archétypes et repétition* (Paris: Gallimard, 1949).

16. All English translations of the *Polyphemus* are from Lowry's study, cited in our note 11, pp. 181–213 (odd numbered pages only). Nelson's translation is quoted by permission of the publisher, copyright © 1961 by Yale University Press. Lowry numbers his stanzas somewhat differently: the introduction is (1)–(3); the narrative proper is 1–60. Dámaso Alonso numbers from 1–63.

17. *Ed. cit.*, pp. 281 ff.

18. C. Colin Smith studies the artistry of this stanza form, typical of the Renaissance repertory in Spain, in two papers, "La musicalidad del 'Polifemo,'" *Revista de filología española*, 44 (1961), 139–66; and "Rich Rhyme in Góngora's *Polifemo*," *Bulletin of Hispanic Studies*, 42 (1965), 104–12.

19. See the definitions given for *bárbaro* in Bernardo Alemany y Selfa, *Vocabulario de las obras de don Luis de Góngora y Argote* (Madrid: Real Academia Española, 1930).

20. We are not sure of Nelson's translation, "Venus leads in her the triad of her graces." According to Alonso's prose version, the meaning is more accurately: Venus has summarized in Galatea the triad of her [i.e., Venus'] graces. Cf. *Ed. cit.*, p. 97.

21. See Dámaso Alonso's notes on this formula in *La lengua poética de Góngora*. 3d. ed. (Madrid: Consejo Superior de Investigaciones Científicas, 1961), pp. 138–56.

22. Oreste Frattoni would have us believe that the story itself is a simple pretext, that, in order to concentrate on stylistic questions, the poet undertakes to effect an "atomization of content." See his *Góngora* (Buenos Aires: Centro Editor de América Latina, 1968), pp. 42 and 44, respectively.

23. While the morphology of the original Spanish is admittedly ambiguous, Nelson unquestionably errs in translating "the sportive vine of his new trunk." The vine is Galatea, and she has entwined herself around *her* new (because of the dramatic transformation in her being) trunk, which is a metaphor for Acis (the sexual symbology of all this hardly needs mention). That our interpretation is more accurate is borne out by the correct translation of the following stanza, where "fear ties her to the unhappy elm."

24. In addition to Alonso's own commentaries, see also papers by Alfonso Reyes, "La estrofa reacia del *Polifemo*," *Nueva revista de filología hispánica*, 7 (1954), 295–306; and by Emilio Carilla, "La estrofa XI del *Polifemo*," *Revista de filología española*, 47 (1964), 369–77. As Alfonso Reyes observes, "we have spent four hundred years arguing about this stanza."

Chapter Five

1. For Pellicer and Díaz de Rivas see the *Soledades*, ed. por Dámaso Alonso. 3d. ed. (Madrid: Sociedad de Estudios y Publicaciones, 1956), pp. 9–10.

2. Robert Jammes, *Études sur l'oeuvre poétique de don Luis de Góngora y Argote* (Bordeaux: Institut d'Études Ibériques et Ibéro-Américaines de l'Université de Bordeaux, 1967), pp. 581–86.

3. Our outline is adapted from Oreste Frattoni, *Góngora* (Buenos Aires: Centro Editor de América Latina, 1968), pp. 48–52. Note that the *First Solitude* is preceded by the separately-numbered stanzas of the Dedication.

4. Among Alonso's studies, those which treat the *Solitudes* are: *La*

lengua poética de Góngora. 3d. ed. (Madrid: Consejo Superior de Investigaciones Científicas, 1961); the edition of the poem cited in note 1; *Cuatro poetas españoles* (Madrid: Gredos, 1962); *Estudios y ensayos gongorinos.* 3d. ed. (Madrid: Gredos, 1970). See also Andrew Debicki, *Dámaso Alonso* (New York: Twayne, 1970), Chapter 4, "Alonso's Critical Works."

5. R. O. Jones, "Neoplatonism and the *Soledades,*" *Bulletin of Hispanic Studies,* 40 (1963), 1–16, discusses the philosophical import of this letter.

6. Luis de Góngora, *Obras completas,* ed. de Juan Millé y Giménez, e Isabel Millé y Giménez. 4th ed. (Madrid: Aguilar, 1956), p. 896. The translation is our own.

7. Góngora, *loc. cit.* The translation is our own.

8. Federico García Lorca, *Obras completas,* ed. de Arturo del Hoyo. 4th ed. (Madrid: Aguilar, 1960), pp. 65–88. The quotes are taken from several passages; the translation is our own.

9. Walter Pabst, *Creación gongorina en los poemas* Polifemo *y* Soledades, trad. de Nicolás Marín (Madrid: Consejo Superior de Investigaciones Científicas, 1966).

10. See Jammes, Chapitre V, "Les Solitudes."

11. R. O. Jones, "Neoplatonism . . . ." Jones also discusses Góngora's vision of mankind and society in "The Poetic Unity of the *Soledades,*" *Bulletin of Hispanic Studies,* 31 (1954), 189–204.

12. Eunice Joiner Gates, "Góngora's *Polifemo* and the *Soledades* in Relation to Baroque Art," *Texas Studies in Language and Literature,* 2 (1960), 6–77.

13. Emilio Orozco Díaz, *En torno a las "Soledades" de Góngora . . .* (Granada: Universidad de Granada, 1969).

14. Maurice Molho, *Sémantique et poétique, à propos des* Solitudes *de Góngora* (Bordeaux: Ducros, 1969).

15. See Luis Muñoz G., "Estructura de *Las Soledades,*" *Atenea,* No. 393 (1968), 179–201.

16. Molho, pp. 49–61.

17. See Pabst, p. 24.

18. All quotes from the original Spanish text are taken from Dámaso Alonso's edition cited in note 1.

19. All English translations of the text are taken from *The Solitudes,* trans. by Gilbert F. Cunningham (Baltimore: The Johns Hopkins Press, 1968).

20. See Pabst, pp. 47 and 48.

Selected Bibliography

PRIMARY SOURCES

1. *Complete Works* (in chronological order)

Obras en verso del Homero español, que recogio Iuan Lopez de Vicuña (Madrid: Viuda de L. Sanchez, 1627). Facsimile edition reprinted, with Prólogo e índices por Dámaso Alonso (Madrid: Consejo Superior de Investigaciones Científicas, 1963).

Todas las obras de Don Lvis de Gongora en varios poemas. Recogidos por Don Gonzalo de Hozes y Cordoua (Madrid: Imprenta del Reino, 1633. Reprinted, 1634. Reprinted, Seuilla: Nicolas Rodriguez, 1648. Reprinted, Madrid: En la Imprenta Real, 1654).

Obras de Don Lvis de Gongora, comentadas por Garcia de Salzedo Coronel (Madrid: Imprenta Real, 1636–48).

Obras poéticas de d. Luis de Góngora . . . , edited by R. Foulché-Delbosc (New York: The Hispanic Society of America, 1921. Reprinted, 1970).

Obras completas de don Luis de Góngora y Argote. Ed. de Juan Millé y Giménez [e] Isabel Millé y Giménez (Madrid: M. Aguilar, 1932. Reprinted, 1943, 1956, 1961, 1967).

2. *Anthologies* (in chronological order)

Poesías escogidas de D. Luis de Góngora y Argote, dadas á luz, corregidas y aumentadas con varias inéditas por D. Luis María Ramírez y las Casas-Deza, entre los Árcades, Ramilio Tartesíaco (Córdoba: Imprenta de Noguér y Manté, 1841).

Poesías; prólogo de Santiago Montoto de Sebas . . . 5th ed. (Madrid: Compañía Ibero-Americana de Publicaciones, 1927?).

Versos de Góngora; en el III centenario del óbito del poeta. Edited by José Priego López (Córdoba: Imp. de "El Previsor," 1927).

Poesías de d. Luis de Góngora y Argote; selección y observaciones preliminares de Eduardo Juliá Martínez. 1st. ed. (Madrid: Hernando, 1929).

Poesía; selección, estudio y notas por J. Manuel Blecua. 1st ed., ilustrada (Zaragoza: Editorial Ebro, 1940. Reprinted, 1960).

Poesías: Polifemo, Soledades, and other poems; edited with introduction by J. W. Barker (Cambridge, Eng.: The University Press, 1942).

Fábula de Polifemo, y otros poemas. Introd. de Jesús Manuel Alda-Tesán. Edición de José Manuel Blecua (Zaragoza: Aula, 1960).

Romances, letrillas, sonetos y canciones. Fragmento de Soledad primera.

Ed. anotada y dispuesta en homenaje al cuarto centenario del nacimiento del poeta. Prólogo y notas de Alicia Galaz Vivar (Santiago de Chile: Editorial Universitaria, 1961).

Poems; selected, introduced and annotated by R. O. Jones (London: Cambridge University Press, 1966).

3. *Ballads* (in chronological order; see also *Anthologies*)

Delicias del Parnaso, en que se cifran todos los romances liricos, amorosos, burlescos, glosas, y decimas satiricas del regosijo de las musas al prodigioso don Luis de Gongora. Recogido todo de sus originales, y corregido de los errores con que estauan corruptos (Barcelona: P. Lacavalleria, y a su costa, 1634. Reprinted 1640 and 1643; title varies slightly).

Romances de Góngora, editados por José María de Cossío (Madrid: Revista de Occidente, 1927).

Píramo y Tisbe. Con los comentarios de Salazar Mardones, y Pellicer, extractados y presentados por A. Rumeau (Paris: Ediciones Hispano-Americanas, 1961).

Romance de Angélica y Medoro; estudio-comentario, versión prosificada y notas por Dámaso Alonso, y tres ilustraciones originales de Gregorio Prieto (Madrid: Ediciones Acies, 1962).

4. *Sonnets* (See also *Anthologies*)

Sonetos completos. Edición, introducción y notas de Biruté Ciplijauskaité (Madrid: Castalia, 1969).

5. *Polifemo* (in chronological order; see also *Anthologies*)

El Polifemo de Don Lvis de Gongora; comentado por Don Garcia de Salzedo Coronel (Madrid: I. Gonçalez, 1629).

Fábula de Polifemo y Galatea. Ed. de A. Reyes (Madrid: Rivadeneyra, 1923).

Góngora y el «Polifemo.» Estudio sobre Góngora y sus obras . . . , comentada en pormenor, primera impresión del texto completo del «Polifemo,» con versión en prosa, comentarios y notas [por] Dámaso Alonso (Madrid: Gredos, 1960. Reprinted, with corrections, etc., 1960, 1961, 1967).

El Polifemo sin lágrimas; la "Fábula de Acis y Galatea." Libre interpretación del texto de Góngora [por] Alfonso Reyes (Madrid: Aguilar, 1961).

6. *Soledades* (in chronological order; see also *Anthologies*)

Soledades. Comentadas por García de Salzedo Coronel (Madrid: Real, 1636?).

Soledades de Góngora, editadas por Dámaso Alonso (Madrid: Revista de Occidente, 1927. Nueva edición, Madrid: Cruz y Raya, 1936. Reprinted, Madrid: Sociedad de Estudios y Publicaciones, 1956).

7. *Theater* (see also *Complete Works*)

Qvatro comedias famosas de Don Lvis de Gongora, y Lope de Vega Carpio, recopiladas por Antonio Sanchez (Madrid: L. S., 1617).

8. *Letrillas* (see also *Anthologies* and *Ballads*)

Letrillas. Texte établi et annoté par Robert Jammes (Paris: Ediciones Hispano-Americanas, 1963).

9. *English Translations* (in alphabetical order by title)

"Fable of Polifemus and Galatea," in Lowry Nelson, Jr., *Baroque Lyric Poetry* (New Haven: Yale University Press, 1961), pp. 180–213 [Nelson's own translation.]

The Solitudes of Don Luis de Gongora, translated into English verse by Edward Meryon Wilson (Cambridge, Eng.: G. Fraser, The Minority Press, 1931. Rev. ed., Cambridge, Eng.: University Press, 1965. Revised and edited by Willis Barnstone, New York: Las Américas, 1965).

The Solitudes of Luis de Góngora. The Spanish text, with an English translation by Gilbert F. Cunningham. Pref. by A. A. Parker. Introd. by Elias L. Rivers (Baltimore: Johns Hopkins Press, 1968). Reprint of a 1964 private edition in Alva, Scotland.

Secondary Sources

(Because of the vast number of studies, this listing must be highly selective, and, with few exceptions, references to analyses of individual compositions are to be found in the notes to the chapters.)

Alemany y Selfa, Bernardo. *Vocabulario de las obras de don Luis de Góngora y Argote* (Madrid: Real Academia Española, 1930). Dictionary compilation of vocabulary of the works, with definitions of the uses of each word.

Alonso, Dámaso. "Alusión y elusión en la poesía de Góngora." In his *Estudios y ensayos gongorinos,* q. v., pp. 92–113 (orig. 1928). Details basic characteristics of allusion and periphrasis as used to "avoid" the common in meaning and reference.

———. *Estudios y ensayos gongorinos.* 3d. ed. (Madrid: Gredos, 1970; orig. 1955). Collection of essays on various aspects of Góngora's language and relations with Renaissance poetic structures; analyses of individual compositions, basically from point of view of style.

———. *La lengua poética de Góngora.* 3d. ed. (Madrid: Consejo Superior de Investigaciones Científicas, 1961; orig. 1935). A major analysis, in schematic form, of most significant aspects of Góngora's poetic language; essential unity of style stressed for all periods of his literary activity.

———. "Los pecadillos de don Luis de Góngora," *Revista de filología española,* 47 (1964), 215–35. Internal evidence from Góngora's works as to his worldly "sins," despite his religious vows, which he appeared never seriously to have kept.

ARTIGAS Y FERRANDO, MIGUEL. *Don Luis de Góngora y Argote, biografía y estudio crítico* (Madrid: Real Academia Española, 1925). Still the most authoritative biography of the poet. See his supplementary note published in *Revista de filología española,* 14 (1927), 404–16.

BODINI, VITTORIO. *Studi sul barroco di Góngora* (Roma: Ateneo, (1964). Essays reprinted here are a reaction to Alonso's placing of G. within a dominantly classical/Renaissance rhetoric; focuses on G.'s thematic and stylistic originality in terms of a uniquely Baroque imagery.

Boletín de la Real Academia de Ciencias, Bellas Letras y Nobles Artes de Córdoba, 6, No. 18 (1927). Entire issue is one of the original 1927 homage volumes for the tricentennial of G.'s death.

BROCKHAUS, E. *Góngoras Sonnettendichtung* (Bochum-Langerdreer: H. Pöppinghaus, 1935). Examination of themes, meanings, sources, and structure of G.'s sonnets, along with typological classification. Particular attention is paid to questions of language and form.

CIOCCHINI, H. *Góngora y la tradición de los emblemas* (Bahia Blanca, Arg.: Universidad Nacional del Sur, 1960). Discusses G.'s use of European, originally didactic, emblematic tradition, understanding emblem here as an emphasis on figurative *explicatio* that conveys a visual image or verbal symbolic hieroglyphic.

COLLARD, ANDRÉE. *Nueva poesía: conceptismo, culteranismo en la crítica española* (Madrid: Castalia, 1967). Central contribution of this study is in terms of the shades of meaning of various critical terms used to describe Spanish seventeenth-century poetry. The second chapter is devoted to criticism of G. in the seventeenth century.

CRAWFORD, J. P. W. "Italian Sources of Góngora's Poetry," *Romanic Review,* 20 (1929), 122–30. Parallels between Góngora and Italian poets, Minturno, Bernardo and Torquato Tasso, Sannazaro in particular.

CURTIUS, ERNST ROBERT. *European Literature and the Latin Middle Ages* (New York: Pantheon Books, 1953; orig. 1948 in German). In addition to many references to Spanish Baroque, see Chapter 15, "Mannerism," especially.

DEHENNIN, ELSA. *La résurgence de Góngora et la génération poétique de 1927* (Paris: Didier, 1962). Discusses resurgence of interest in G. against the background of earlier negative judgments; focus is on both critical interest as well as influence on poetry of early twentieth century.

FOULCHÉ-DELBOSC, RAYMOND. "Bibliographie de Góngora," *Revue his-*

panique, 18 (1908), 73–161. Arrangement is by date of original composition of divulgation, 1580–1906.

FRATTONI, ORESTE. *Ensayo para una historia del soneto en Góngora* (Buenos Aires: Universidad de Buenos Aires, Facultad de Filosofía y Letras, 1948). Traces developmental lines of G.'s sonnets, with particular emphasis on style and technique, taking the form of a brief, and at times quite superficial, commentary on texts in chronological order.

———. *Góngora* (Buenos Aires: Centro Editor de América Latina, 1968). Useful, if all too brief, introduction to the poet and the general issues of his work.

GARCIA LORCA, FEDERICO. "La imagen poética de don Luis de Góngora," *Residencia*, 4 (1932), 94–100. Also reprinted in various editions of Lorca's *Obras completas*. Significant appreciation by a major poet of the Generation of 1927 of the aesthetic value of G.'s metaphoric art.

GATES, EUNICE JOINER. "Góngora's *Polifemo* and *Soledades* in Relation to Baroque Art," *Texas Studies in Literature and Language*, 2 (1960), 61–77. Attempt at defining "Baroque" as manifested in G.'s two major works. Special reference is made to the plastic arts and Wölfflin's famous hypotheses.

———. *The Metaphors of Luis de Góngora* (Philadelphia: University of Pennsylvania Press, 1933). By focusing on G.'s metaphors—and on his metaphorical language in general—Gates details in considerable depth the poet's development of a literary style that would rival Latin as a literary vehicle.

GOIC, CEDOMIL. "Góngora y la retórica manierista de la dificultad docta," *Atenea*, No. 393 (1961), 168–78. Considers Baroque modifications in Aristotelian dictum of elevated style and clarity of diction; Baroque writers and theoreticians elaborated on the concept of a high style for Spanish.

GRISMER, RAYMOND L. "Classical Allusions in the Poetic Works of Góngora," *Hispania*, 30 (1947), 496–504. Adopts rather negative attitude toward G.'s understanding of classical myths, assuming a virtue in faithful reconstructions rather than the poet's unique uses to his own ends.

GUILLÉN, JORGE. "Poetic Language: Góngora." In his *Language and Poetry* (Cambridge: Harvard University Press, 1961), pp. 25–75. Another poet of the Generation of 1927 expresses appreciation for G.'s achievements in his Eliot Norton lectures at Harvard.

HATZFELD, HELMUT. "The Baroque of Cervantes and the Baroque of Góngora," *Anales Cervantinos*, 3 (1953), 87–119. Cervantes is more truly "Baroque," while G. is better understood as Mannerist, an assertion demonstrated by points of diversion as well as contact between major works of the two contemporaries.

———. "El manierismo de Góngora en la *Soledad Primera*," *Atenea*, No. 363 (1961), 47–55. Additional notes on the problem with specific reference to the *Soledades*.

JAMMES, ROBERT. *Études sur l'oeuvre poétique de Don Luis de Góngora y Argote* (Bordeaux: Institut d'Études Ibériques et Ibéro-Américaines de l'Université de Bordeaux, 1967). A major study tracing developmental trajectory of the poetry in terms of G. as a rebellious spokesman of his age. Essentially downgrades courtly poetry and tends to see long narrative poems as the crowning achievement, with emphasis also on the satirico-burlesque compositions.

JONES, R. O. "Góngora and Neoplatonism Again," *Bulletin of Hispanic Studies*, 43 (1966), 117–20. Reaffirmation of position in 1963 article, in answer to Smith's refutation in 1965 article.

———. "Neoplatonism and the *Soledades*," *Bulletin of Hispanic Studies*, 40 (1963), 1–16. Examination of the *Soledades* as indicative of major intellectual preoccupations of Renaissance Neoplatonism. See Smith's 1965 article.

LEFEBVRE, ALFREDO. "Lugares poéticos de Góngora," *Atenea*, No. 393 (1961), 149–67. Treats two antithetical commonplaces in G.'s sonnets: the pathetic "guilt" of an autobiographical piece and the erotic cliché of woman's "hair of gold" as seen in a few poems and love sonnets.

LORING, S. *La poesía religiosa de don Luis de Góngora* (Córdoba: Colegio Noviciado San Francisco de Borja, 1962). Not available for our examination.

LOVELUCK M., JUAN. "Un motivo de la espiritualidad barroca en la poesía de Góngora," *Atenea*, No. 393 (1961), 242–59. Brief comparison of G.'s Baroque "spirituality" with general characteristics of period; G. is seen as more "pre-Baroque" and lacking Quevedo's philosophic concerns.

MOLHO, MAURICE. *Sémantique et poétique: à propos des* Solitudes *de Góngora* (Bordeaux: Ducros, 1969). Reproduction of 1960 article preceded by extensive theoretical introduction. M.'s approach, via current semantic theories, focuses on G.'s creation of a unique field of poetic meaning from base semantics of nonpoetic language.

———. "Soledades," *Bulletin hispanique*, 62 (1960), 249–85. See preceding entry.

MÜLLER, B. *Góngoras Metaphorik. Versuch einer Typologie* (Wiesbaden: Franz Steiner, 1963). Not available for our examination.

OROZCO DÍAZ, EMILIO. "Estructura manierista y estructura barroca en la poesía. Introducción y comentarios a unos sonetos de Góngora."

In *Historia y estructura de la obra literaria*... (Madrid: Consejo Superior de Investigaciones Científicas, 1971), pp. 97–115. Accepting validity of distinction between Mannerist (post-Renaissance intellectual and stylistic instability, disharmony) and Baroque (new synthesis of Renaissance and Mannerist), O. proceeds to demonstrate presence of both strands in G.'s sonnets, relating their structural complexity to Mannerism.

———. *Góngora* (Barcelona: Labor, 1950). Good general introduction with anthology; valuable for survey of criticism.

PABST, WALTER. *La creación gongorina en los poemas* Polifemo *y* Soledades (Madrid: Consejo Superior de Investigaciones Científicas, 1966; orig. 1930 in German). Pabst's study, along with Dámaso Alonso's early essays, represented one of the first attempts to "prove" conclusively G.'s artistic merits.

PAIEWONSKY CONDE, EDGAR. "Góngora y la visión del mundo como posibilidad," *Cuadernos hispanoamericanos*, No. 202 (1966), 62–88. Most important aspect is a questioning of post-1927 criticism and a reevaluation of focus of eighteenth- and nineteenth-century commentaries. An enthusiastic evaluation of G.'s poetry is proposed from point of view of obscurity, vacuousness, and "visionary madness." Discussion of G.'s preoccupation with the "possible" rather than the "actual."

PENNY, CLARA LOUISA. *Luis de Góngora y Argote* (New York: Hispanic Society of America, 1926). General presentation, although somewhat outdated and overly biographical. Of interest as early treatise in English.

PÉREZ, CARLOS A. "Juegos de palabras y formas de engaño en la poesía de don Luis de Góngora," *Hispanófila*, No. 20 (1964), 5–47; No. 21 (1964), 41–72. Systematic study of G.'s use of "confusion and obfuscation" as aesthetic phenomena that function to produce aesthetic pleasure in the perceptive reader.

REYES, ALFONSO. "Cuestiones gongorinos." In his *Obras completas* (México: Fondo de Cultura Económica, 1955), VII, 10–167 (orig. 1927). This and following item are series of minor essays on diverse aspects of G.'s work by the great Mexican humanist.

———. "Tres alcances a Góngora." In his *Obras completas, ed. cit.*, VII, 169–232 (orig. 1945 and 1954).

SALEMBIEN, L. "Góngora," *Bulletin hispanique*, 31 (1929), 293–330; 32 (1930), 114–84. Early monographic presentation in French.

SALINAS, PEDRO. "The Exaltation of Reality: Luis de Góngora." In his *Reality and the Poet in Spanish Poetry* (Baltimore: Johns Hopkins Press, 1940), pp. 129–47. S. is neither literary critic nor theoretician, but his sympathetic comments to the general reader as poet of the 1927 group characterize G.'s *Soledades* as "superreality exaggerated and exalted."

SAN JUAN, E., JR. "Contiguity and Similarity as Poetic Modes in Some Poems of Góngora," *Kentucky Foreign Language Quarterly*, 13 (1966), 43–50. Jakobsen's concept of metonymy and metaphor are used to discuss G.'s poetic constants. Contiguity refers to meanings suggested for items by their co-occurrence in a context.

SÁNCHEZ, LUIS ALBERTO. "Aspectos de lo cómico en la poesía de Góngora," *Revista de filologia española*, 44 (1961), 95–138. Focuses on humorous elements in the satirico-burlesque compositions.

SMITH, C. COLIN. "An Approach to Góngora's *Polifemo*," *Bulletin of Hispanic Studies*, 42 (1965), 217–38. Rejecting Jones's 1963 article on Neoplatonism in G.'s major poems, S. stresses how the *Polifemo* deals more with man's place in Nature. See Jones's reply, 1966.

———. "La musicalidad del *Polifemo*," *Revista de filología española*, 44 (1961), 139–66. Attempts to demonstrate G.'s success in being "musical" in his verbal art.

———. "Rich Rhyme in Góngora's *Polifemo*," *Bulletin of Hispanic Studies*, 42 (1965), 104–12. Extends preceding study by focusing on exploitation of aspects of poem's strophic form.

THOMAS, LUCIEN-PAUL. *Góngora et le gongorisme considérés dans leurs rapports avec le marinisme* (Paris: H. Champion, 1911). Early valuable essay on the relationship between G. and Marinist poetry in Italy. Contrary to view that latter influenced former, T. argues the now current view that Spain influenced Italy. G.'s poetry, then, derives basically from a Spanish tradition of complex backgrounds.

UHRHAN, EVELYN ESTHER. "Linguistic Analysis of Góngora's Baroque Style." In H. R. Kahane, and A. Pietrangeli, *Descriptive Studies in Spanish Grammar* (Urbana: University of Illinois Press, 1954), pp. 177–241. Subjects syntax of first *Solitude* to a purely linguistic analysis in order to isolate methodologically six Baroque stylistic "principals." It is not certain how much more than trivial this study is, as all questions of aesthetics are ignored.

VILANOVA, ANTONIO. *Las fuentes y los temas del* Polifemo *de Góngora* (Madrid: Consejo Superior de Investigaciones Científicas, 1957). Exhaustive study of all literary backgrounds, influences, contacts, etc., relating to G.'s *Polifemo*. A major, if somewhat overwhelmingly exhaustive contribution.

WELLEK, RENÉ. "The Concept of Baroque in Literary Scholarship." In his *Concepts of Criticism* (New Haven: Yale University Press, 1963, pp. 69–127; orig. 1946). Major survey of opinions and controversies in scholarship on the Baroque.

Index

(Notes and Bibliography are excluded; Góngora's works that are discussed in this study are entered under their original Spanish title with cross references)

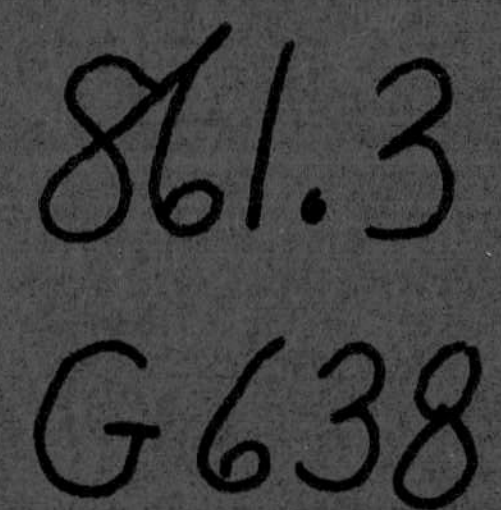